Livin'
Large

Livin'
Large

African American Sisters
Confront Obesity

Stacy Ann Mitchell, M.D. and Teri D. Mitchell

Hilton Publishing Company   Roscoe, IL

Published by Hilton Publishing Company, Inc.
PO Box 737
Roscoe, IL 61073
815-885-1070
www.hiltonpub.com

Publisher's Cataloging -in-Publication
(Provided by Quality Books, Inc.)

Mitchell, Stacy Ann.
    Livin' large : African American sisters confront obesity / Stacy Ann
Mitchell and Teri D. Mitchell.
    p. cm.

    1. Obesity in women. 2. African American women—Health and hygiene.
I. Mitchell, Teri D. II. Title.

RC628.M57 2004   616.3'98'008996073
                                         QBI04-200183

Printed and bound in the United States of America

Contents

Acknowledgments

God is good all the time.

He gave us our family, without whose love and genetics this book never would have been possible.

Mommy: Everything we are is because you were first.

Daddy: You've taught us the value of eternal optimism. We know by your example that when things don't go as planned, you can still take what's been learned and create something great.

Brandon, Brea, Debra: You all are something wonderful!

Granny: Our moral compass . . . you've given us our biggest gifts-one of which is the value of always loving unconditionally.

Grandy: We thank you for our love of learning and aspirations to excellence.

Pops and the Brooks clan: Your love has made us feel so much like members of your family that we really believe we are! We are.

Aunt Bill and NiNi: We learned how to be sisters by watching you be sisters. Thank you for teaching us kindness and generosity.

The Roberts and Logan "kids": What a joy it is to have cousins that are as good as any siblings!

And to Granddaddy and Papa: You were our shining examples of what black men are at their best. We hope there are copies of this book in heaven, and we hope we've made you proud.

To our friends:

We have been blessed to have always been surrounded by beautiful, supportive, loving friends. You've been shoulders to cry on and laugh with. You've given us places that were safe and places where we were accepted and always, always loved. You are part of our family. You know who you are. We are eternally grateful.

Sylvia: Titi loves you.

To Bert Stern, Tom Woll, and everyone at Hilton Publishing: Without your knowledge, encouragement, and help, this never would have gotten done. You have the patience of saints. Thank you for taking a chance on us!

And all the time, God is good. To HIM, we simply say THANKS.

Prologue   *Why This Book? Why Us? Why Now?*

Livin' Large began in a spirit of humor and understanding, in a conversation between sisters. We hope that this same tone, and the information we give you, will take you, our reader, through a journey of self-awareness, knowledge, and greater empowerment.

But that journey must start with your taking in a hard fact. Black women (and men, too) are dying needlessly from diabetes and heart disease and high blood pressure. We are dying from strokes. We are dying because we are too fat.

Contrary to common belief among us, being "too fat" is a disease, just like cancer or tuberculosis or smallpox. The only difference between fat and the diseases just mentioned is that fat kills more often. You need to know that, and so does the community.

According to recent statistics, more than 300,000 people die from obesity-related diseases every year.[1] The percentage of

---

1. Source: Centers for Disease Control and the U.S. Surgeon General

African Americans in that number is disproportionately high. The statistical bad news doesn't end there: over 65 percent of black women are overweight or obese, making them targets of disability and early death. And just one final statistic, to make clear that the economic burden that lies on our community by bad health related to obesity is staggering: the cost to treat the complications of obesity in blacks now tops $30 billion a year.

Far too few of us African American women have taken in these urgent facts. Now, *Livin' Large* gives you the information you need about

- Controlling obesity and staying healthy
- What to ask your doctor when you've been diagnosed with obesity-related illness
- How to meet your goals for a healthy weight and general good health.

What makes us qualified to talk about this subject? Quite simply, *we are just like you*. In *Livin' Large*, we share with you the conversations we've had on this issue of weight- some pleasant and some not so pleasant. Like our conversations with each other, our talk is frank and honest, but it always comes out of love. We're biological sisters . . . but we hope you'll take the opportunity to join our extended family.

We're inviting you to sit with us for a bit and have a real conversation about a very important and sometimes-uncomfortable issue, a conversation that just might save your life or the life of someone you love. In fact, it's our hope that we'll *all* be better and healthier for being part of this conversation.

Livin' Large

Part *One*

How We Got This Way

Chapter One   From "Us" to "You"[2]

First, I would like to congratulate you. By picking up this book you acknowledge that there is a health problem of epidemic proportions in the Black community, and that problem is obesity. Obesity threatens our lives and our community, although, up to now, we haven't done a very good job of addressing it. But that failure can change now, reader by reader.

Obesity is a complicated matter by itself, but when you add the surrounding issues of culture, race, and self-image, it becomes overwhelming. As a doctor, I, Stacy, see the results of obesity every day, in death and disability caused by a disease that's 100 percent treatable and preventable. Yes, I used the term disease. For that is what obesity is, a chronic disease that can be fatal. And, as with most diseases, African Americans suffer more than other races from its harmful effects.

---

2. In the dialogue that follows, Stacy's voice will appear in regular type and Teri's in italics.

One of the difficulties in combating obesity has been our attitude that weight is an aesthetic issue. Let's be clear, it is not. We have been fooled into believing that our body size is what determines our beauty and worth. In our community, "thick" is often considered better and more attractive than "thin." However, if it were just a matter of what society finds visually pleasing, there would be no need for this book.

The absolute truth is that being overweight is dangerous. It's that simple. If you doubt that fact now, keep reading! Obesity is directly associated with the major killers in the African-American community-diabetes, heart disease, and stroke, and obesity is implicated in still another way: there is growing evidence that it contributes to the development of cancer. Worse yet, there is a rapidly growing number of overweight and obese African-American children with potentially dangerous health conditions previously seen only in middle-aged adults.

Unfortunately, the African American community falls prey to a multitude of chronic illnesses, many of them, at least in part, self-induced because of a lack of knowledge. Our goal is to convince you that being obese is a choice. We want to give you and, yes, the community, too, the knowledge and the resolution to make better decisions about your health. Our faith is that once people are given the facts in a straightforward, understandable manner, they will do just that.

Many years ago, Lao-tse, the author of the oldest existing book of Taoism, wrote: "A thousand mile journey starts with one step." You have made that first step, and we think you'll find the following journey exciting. What is so exciting about fat and disease? Simply this: gaining knowledge that lets you take control of your bodies and your health, and allows you to communicate with physicians and other health professionals from the powerful position of an "educated consumer"—now *that's* exciting.

And it doesn't stop there. It is our hope that you'll find that this new "self-determination" only starts with your body. Before long, it will quickly spread to involve other aspects of your life and community.

Now is the time for us, as African Americans, to get real about our health. As a community, we must take a long, hard look at our habits, our self-destructive behaviors, and ourselves, and recognize that we are not the helpless victims of disease and illness. The power to alter the course of our lives is within each of us. Learning to use that power won't be easy, but nothing truly worthwhile ever is.

So, congratulations. You've made one step, and it's a big one.

Did she just say what I think she said—"Congratulations"? Leave it to Stacy to congratulate someone who is about to begin on the toughest uphill battle in the history of medical science. We can find new cures and new tests, transplant organs, and map the human genome, but we can't get people to lose weight.

Oh, excuse me for being rude. I forgot to introduce myself. My name is Teri, and yes, "Doctor Stacy" is my sister. I love her, honest to God I do, but the truth is, she's never had an extra pound in her life. Yep, she's the size 6, skinny girl you sometimes just want to tie a few cement blocks to and toss into the nearest river—especially as you watch her devour a plate of macaroni and cheese. I, on the other hand, am a "recovering big girl," and I have a feeling that Stacy had me in mind when she decided to write this book.

For years, I put up with her endless sermons about my weight and what lies ahead for me if I persist in eating myself into an early grave. But come on, she's my younger sister. I'm supposed to be telling her how to live her life, not the other way around.

But the truth is that I've finally begun to listen to her. And if you are still reading, then maybe you've decided to listen to her as well. Good move. That decision could save your life or the life of a loved one.

Notice how the words "decision" and "choice" keep popping up in our conversation? Admittedly, this was a concept that did not originally set too well with me. I never considered my being big a choice. It just seemed like a given. I saw it as I saw any other physical condition. Some people are tall, some have a clubfoot, some—like me—are "big-boned." I honestly felt I didn't have much say in the matter. This was the way God made me, end of story. I was just "thick."

To complicate the issue, I was cute. That's right—regardless of the excess poundage, I looked good. And as many of you probably already realize, in our community, as black men see it, "thick" is better than thin any day.

Today I realize that I'm as beautiful at a healthy weight as I was at an unhealthy one. And so are you. I found that the trick is to look into the mirror today and be happy with what you see. And then wake up tomorrow and look in the mirror and be happy with what you see. Once you can do that, you're well on your way toward change.

All our hang-ups and issues about weight and body image, and about what's "cute" and what's not, is the wrong motivation, and not the topic of this book. No matter how good we look, if we're not fit and healthy on the inside, we're cheating ourselves. If we can't run and play with our kids because we don't have the lung capacity to run, or can't dance all night with our girlfriends because our knees hurt, or make love all morning with our partners because we tire too quickly, then our quality of life is compromised and we must do something about it.

My sister told me I would make a beautiful corpse. She got my attention. I hope I have yours.

I hope that we can make this change together. I've given some thought to how we can make this journey a bit more enjoyable and a lot easier to swallow. Why don't we do this: I'm going to tag along throughout this book, and when the good Doctor gets a little carried away (which she will do, believe me- I grew up with the girl, remember?), I'll cut in and give the "real deal," one "recovering big girl" to another. This way, you, the reader, can take in all the medical information that truly is vital to living a productive, healthy life. And we just may have a few laughs and learn a little something about ourselves in the process.

So here we go. Welcome to Livin' Large, and I'll talk to you again soon.

Chapter Two

Are You "Fat" or "Fine"? or, "It Must Be My Thyroid" and Other Myths About Obesity

If you've ever been described as "big boned," "chunky," or "thick," you are not alone. In fact, you are in big company (pardon my pun), and your party is growing every day. Obesity is epidemic in this country, and among African Americans its prevalence is even more shocking. Conservative estimates show that among non-Hispanic blacks in the United States, 33 percent of men and a startling 65 percent of women are overweight! Some studies put those percentages even higher, but what is not up for debate is that we are dying in enormous numbers because of obesity.

Obesity is a chronic disease. If you take nothing else with you from this book and decide to read no further, at least take this: obesity is a disease. How, you may ask, can something like the size of your body be categorized as a disease? Consider the definition of disease and the answer becomes clear. Disease is defined as "a condition of an organism that impairs normal physiological functioning." (You are the organism, and "physiological functioning" is fancy talk for how your body works.) And that is what obesity does—by altering the way your body functions, it leads to life-threatening illnesses and even death.

If you take nothing else with you from this book and decide to read no further, at least take this: obesity is a disease.

The terms obesity and overweight are often used interchangeably, but they don't mean exactly the same thing. Obesity is medically defined as "an increase in body fat," but the simplest definition is that obesity is an extreme form of being overweight. A person who is overweight is running a definite health risk, but an obese person is loudly and insistently asking for medical trouble.

The way doctors decide whether you are overweight, or obese, is through a formula that defines the "Body Mass Index," or BMI. The simple way of thinking about it is, how much weight do you carry in proportion to your height? To get the number on the BMI index, use the following formula:

$$BMI = \frac{Weight\ in\ Pounds}{(Height\ in\ inches) \times (Height\ in\ inches) \times 703}$$

But if numbers aren't your thing, don't worry. Your doctor ordinarily calculates your BMI during your checkups, or you can do it for yourself on the internet by going to www.nhlbisupport.com/bmi/. A BMI of 20 to 25 is considered a good weight for most people. "Overweight" is technically defined as a BMI greater than 27, and "obesity" is a BMI greater than 30. A woman who is 5'3" and weighs 150 pounds has a BMI of 26.6, and is very close to being overweight. If she weighed 170 pounds, she'd be indexed at 30.1, or obese.

Some African Americans believe that the standards used in defining obesity are European standards and should not apply to people of color. Indeed, that false belief is one reason why we're not being diagnosed for weight problems and treated for them. If this book were about standards of beauty, perhaps this notion of a different standard for black people would make sense. But in fact it's about standards that mean the difference between life and death.

If you look at the BMI index, you'll see that there is a large "healthy" weight range for each height. That means, within your healthy range, you still have the flexibility to choose a weight where you look good, you feel good, and you're at optimal health.

That said, we want you to completely understand that weight is not an issue of beauty. It is a medical issue. This cannot be stressed enough. The people who came up with the BMI formula weren't interested in defining what was visually stimulating or pleasing. The numbers 27 and 30 were not arbitrarily chosen. They are used because they are the proven levels of BMI at which the risks and incidence of life-threatening diseases such as heart disease and diabetes occur. Fat is dangerous, plain and simple. Trust your BMI to tell you how dangerous fat is for you.

"It MUST Be My Thyroid!" aka "Why I'm Fat"

The causes of obesity continue to be hotly debated among health professionals, scientists, self-proclaimed "weight loss experts," and just about anyone with an opinion and a weight problem. Medicine is never exact, and there remains a lot to be learned about what determines body size. However, there is a lot that we do know about what you inherit from your parents and what you do not.

Overall body size *does* seem to be genetically determined. This means that whether you are small, medium, or large-framed is inherited from your parents, just as you inherit height or eye color. Oprah Winfrey will never be the size of Ally McBeal. It's just not in her genetic makeup. And Ally will never be the size of Oprah, regardless of how much she eats.

But while your genes incline you to a general body size, being obese is not the fault of your DNA. Within each body size, there is a range of healthy weight. Except in *extremely* rare genetic disorders, children are not born to be obese.

If you take in more calories than you burn off, you will gain weight.

What causes people to be fat, after we're done with all the technical stuff, is very simple: If you take in more calories than you burn off, you will gain weight. Lots of people have made lots of dollars trying to convince us otherwise, but the fact still remains and it holds true for *everyone*—skinny people and fat people alike.

Here's how it works. When you consume, for example, 2,600 calories in a day (which is equivalent to a fast food cheeseburger and fries), but you use up only 1,500 calories in activity for that day, the extra 1,100 calories is stored as fat. That's the clear, hard truth.

What I hear from some of my patients is: "But Dr. Mitchell, everyone in my family is fat. It has to be genetic!" The bitter truth is that what you inherited from your family was your eating habits. While you were growing up, you likely ate the same things mom and dad ate, and this was the same diet that made them overweight. Common sense dictates that this would make you overweight as well.

By now, you have met my dear sister, Teri. She's a lovely girl, but I must be honest. She was the motivation for the title of this chapter. For years, Teri insisted that the root of her weight problem was an under-active thyroid. And she is by no means alone. If I had a dollar for each obese patient who insisted that there must be some "glandular" problem, this book would have been written from the deck of my yacht! In blaming the poor, defenseless thyroid for weight disorders, what most patients are trying to do, but not very successfully, is to understand the concept of metabolism.

What Is Metabolism?

The term *metabolism* refers to the body's process of breaking down food in order to make energy. Metabolism is a complex interaction between factors such as hormones, calorie intake, activity level, and muscle mass. Having an underactive thyroid gland may slow metabolism, and it may even cause some amount of weight gain, usually five to ten pounds, mostly due to water retention. However, this condition is *not* a widespread cause of obesity. A simple blood test done by your doctor can quickly diagnose a thyroid disorder, and a small pill taken daily can

> *Metabolism is a complex interaction between factors such as hormones, calorie intake, activity level, and muscle mass.*

replace the hormone if it is low. So the vast majority of you must cross your glands off of the "why I'm fat" list.

Everyone's metabolism is different. For example, each of us uses a certain number of calories when at complete rest (as when sitting and watching television). This is called the "basal metabolic rate." That term refers to the number of calories burned each day just to sustain the body's basic functions, such as breathing and heartbeat.

Some of us are "metabolically gifted" and use up large amounts of calories doing nothing. Others are more "metabolically challenged" and require more activity in order to burn the same number of calories that the more "gifted" can use up just sitting on the couch.

While your genes play a part in determining which category you fall into, so does your age. The older you get, the slower your metabolism becomes. But the story does not end there. No matter what your body type and age, you can do things to make your body a more effective calorie-burning machine. Knowing and doing those things is the key to effective, lasting weight loss and good health.

> *The first way to improve your metabolism is to increase your level of physical activity.*

The first way to improve your metabolism is to increase your level of physical activity. Get used to hearing about exercise, even if it's not what you want to hear. Exercise is essential to any serious effort at winning and maintaining better health.

Exercise increases your metabolic rate (i.e., the speed at which you burn calories) in three ways.

The first way is the most obvious. You directly burn more calories when you engage in physical activity. For example, a brisk, thirty-minute walk will directly consume roughly 200 calories.

The second way that exercise increases your metabolic rate is that your metabolism remains higher for a period as long as twelve to sixteen hours *after* the physical activity. Therefore, the food you eat throughout the day is more efficiently broken down into energy instead of fat.

The third way exercise helps metabolism is by increasing lean muscle mass. Muscle burns calories more effectively and more rapidly than fat.

A second important way to enhance metabolism (are you ready for this one?) is to eat regularly. Yep, you read it correctly. Skipping meals and not eating enough food decreases your metabolism. Think of it this way. Let's imagine a child whose parents provide an allowance of ten dollars a week. Each Monday, the child picks up the ten dollars, and if the money is budgeted wisely it will last until the next Sunday. Now, what would happen if on Monday the child went to receive her ten dollars but was sent away empty-handed and told to try again next week? She would wait until the next week rolls around and, happily, she gets her ten dollars.

But now she is no longer certain that she can rely on the weekly inflow of cash. She may get more money for next week, or she might not see her next allowance for another two or maybe even three weeks. So, wisely, she budgets her money and spends it less quickly, since she is unsure how long it must last.

This is exactly what your body does when it is faced with an extremely restricted diet. Since it doesn't know for certain when the next meal is coming, your metabolism goes into "starvation mode"—that is, it slows down and "budgets" the calories more tightly. In that way, your body tries to hold on to every calorie you take in for as long as possible. Calories end up being stored away as fat instead of being burned off as energy. The way to avoid this is by eating regular, balanced meals (more on this later).

In a Nutshell

All overweight and obese people either:

- Eat too much
- Exercise too little
- Or both (It's usually both)

There's no magic in the way you got overweight, and there's no magic to the way you can slim down. Sure, every day there's a new diet book that claims to be the key to that magic, a "secret formula," drug, or method that will make you slim without much effort on your part. The black community more than any other group has fallen prey to these schemes. But it's all smoke and mirrors. You are fat because of what you do or don't do. Eating too much and exercising too little are the key reasons why you have a problem. That may sound harsh, but it's the truth. Better to live with that truth than to be taken in by sucker schemes that may be useless or even dangerous to your health.

Hello again. It's me, Teri.

Doc Stacy has done a lot in bringing me to the painful realization that my own choices are the root of my weight problem. But she also makes me see that the solution to my problem doesn't rest entirely on science. We have to look into ourselves to discover why we eat so much, why we fail to exercise, why we slowly commit suicide each day at the neighborhood fast food restaurant. It is not the understanding of hormone levels, muscle mass, or the physiology of metabolism and biochemical processes that will lead us to better health.

Ultimately, we must understand ourselves.

Here's a poem that helped me to see myself clearly and to understand. I hope it will help you, too.

The Heart of the Fat

My happiness is smothered in gravy.
My tears are sugarcoated and dipped in chocolate.
My boredom finds escape in a beer-battered fish fry.
My elation finds heaven buried under the golden arches.
My sadness at life and circumstances is swimming in
       butter.
I yearn for the comfort and safety of home,
of granny,
Of being rocked to sleep in a soft mound of lilac scented
       flesh.
I crave control over a world spinning crazily towards chaos.
So I eat.
And smile.
And feel good for the moment.
Hunger is foreign never having a chance to get its foot in
       the door
Before another need quickly surfaces
And must be satisfied
With peach cobbler.

Did you recognize yourself in this like I did? Good! Keep reading.

Chapter Three   *Why Do You Eat? The Psychological Dimension*

Let me tell you about a patient who was introduced to me in the fall of 2002. We'll call her Lisa. Lisa came to my office one Friday afternoon. She was late about forty-five minutes late—for the last appointment of the day. And I had been looking forward to this particular weekend since last Monday so, as you can probably guess, Doctor Stacy was not a happy camper.

As I glanced at my new patient's chart before entering the examination room, one thing in particular caught my eye. Her weight was recorded as "400 +." My first thought was "plus what?" Then I entered the room to finally meet Lisa, my late, 400-plus, keeping-me-from-my-dinner-date patient. At that moment I'd never have guessed that Lisa would forever change the way I looked at obesity—not just the disease itself, but the life and the struggles that went with it.

When Lisa came into the examination room, her husband and son came in with her. But I hardly noticed them at first because Lisa commanded the room. To be blunt, she was big.

Huge. Massive even. She was leaning against the examination table because she could not fit in any of the seats and she could not lift herself up onto the table.

Lisa was upfront about why and how she ended up in my office. Her husband had made an appointment for her several months ago that she did not keep. Now he threatened to leave her if she did not see a doctor. Lisa's experiences with doctors in the past had left her more disheartened and hopeless than ever. She said that I was the last doctor she would agree to see, and she swore to her husband that if she once again left hurt and ashamed, she would never step foot in another physician's office. In other words, she would simply accept the fact that she would likely die soon, and would not attempt to do anything about it.

I was a little intimidated and also a bit angry. Who was this woman, this stranger, to put all the responsibility for her health and her life of thirty-eight years on my shoulders when she just met me? How dare she? But I kept listening, and I'm glad I did.

Lisa went on to tell me a little bit about her life. She was married, and that was her only son, Kendy, age five, who was now in the waiting room with her husband. Her husband, by the way, was supportive, loving, deeply concerned, and all of 150 pounds dripping wet. No derogatory word about her weight had ever come from his lips in their entire twenty years together. He was her high-school sweetheart, and had been there from her "brick house" size-eight days to the point where she was now, and through all the ups and downs in between.

At this point, I'd removed the white coat, taken a seat, and accepted the fact that it was going to be a late evening. But I also realized something: I was starting to really like this woman. I felt something special for her, like I needed to protect her in some way. Maybe I was still taken aback by the way she had been treated by physicians in the past and I wanted to "redeem" my profession.

I made a few half-hearted attempts to ask all the "medical" questions, but the conversation would quickly turn back to Lisa and her life. She interrupted me because she wanted me to know, before we went any further, that she was a good person. She was not lazy or nasty. She cared about her family and she worked hard at her job, even though she lived with unspeakable discomfort because of her obesity.

The fact that Lisa felt the need to say those words to me spoke volumes about the depth, complexity, and pain of her situation. No patient had ever felt obligated to justify themselves to me unprovoked and unsolicited. But I figured that this is what she felt the need to do with everyone she met. If that didn't just about make me weep, what followed certainly did.

Lisa felt that her problems began after the death of her mother two years before. She said that she gained 140 pounds soon after she lost her mother due to heart failure and complications from diabetes. She believed that the depression that followed the loss of her mother and best friend caused her to overeat and become self-destructive. She even admitted that there was a bit of "self-fulfilling prophecy" involved. Since her mother died due to obesity-related illness, Lisa was perhaps trying, though unconsciously, to hasten her own death by the same means.

At this point, I interrupted Lisa, because although the death of her mother was an easy and logical reason for the extreme obesity, even without the additional 140 pounds, she had weighed 300 pounds before this upheaval. I was quick to bring this up because I didn't want to let my new favorite patient leave my office that day thinking she had convinced me that her problems started only two years ago. In fact, as it turned out, the death of Lisa's mother was only the tip of an iceberg that had its roots way back in childhood.

Your weight history, in simplest form, is your lowest weight as an adult, how much you weighed as a teenager, and whether you have had any success losing weight in the past.

When I asked her weight history—questions such as what was her lowest weight as an adult, how much she weighed as a teenanger, and had she had success losing weight in the past—something telling came up. Lisa started to gain weight in high school, around the age of fifteen, and the reason was not random. A year earlier, an uncle she had known and trusted all of her life had molested her. Things went downhill from there.

Lisa kept the secret to herself, as most children do. She believed her uncle when he said that no one would think she was telling the truth and she would destroy the family if she opened her mouth. Tragically, this violation of her body and her trust occurred at the same point in her life that her self-image and sexuality were beginning to develop. The 400-plus pound result of this was now sitting in my office. And it was devastating.

Looking back, Lisa could see that, unconsciously at the time, she began to gain a lot of weight because it made her feel safe. Lisa did not want to be attractive or be perceived as a sexual person in any way. In short, she wanted to disappear. In her mind, fat allowed her to slip in under the radar of her uncle in particular, and of men in general. Fat gave her a kind of anonymity, which allowed her to cope with growing into womanhood under such deplorable conditions. Back then, in her teens, Lisa didn't see that her uncle was sick. He had the perverted need to control innocent girls, and her abuse had nothing to do with how thin or how pretty she was. Now, as an adult, Lisa had a better grasp on why she was put through such horror. But the damage had already been done.

After giving me that history, Lisa began to tell me about how she felt on a daily basis; she knew these feelings had their roots in the past. She said she was disgusted with herself for letting things get so out of control. At the same time, she felt hopeless to improve things. She couldn't see past her present physical and emotional situation.

Every day, as she dressed herself, she saw each roll of fat as a symbol of her weakness and her failure as a mother, wife, and human being. She could barely walk because of her weight, she had not made love to her husband in three years, and her son barely recognize his mother outside the context of the sofa. She rarely left the house anymore, and she spent most waking hours daydreaming about the day when she would find a bit of peace. Obviously, Lisa was in deep pain. And what did she do when the pain became too much? She ate. Many of you might recognize parts of yourselves or a loved one in Lisa's story.

Having Lisa as my patient taught me how complicated the subject of obesity is, and how there are many psychological and psychiatric issues that must be addressed before any degree of long-term good health can be yours. Putting someone on a low-calorie diet and an exercise program is the easy part. Changing the pathologic relationship with food and the self-destructive patterns of behavior that are often a part of obesity—that is where the real challenge lies.

So Why Do You Eat?

When it's all said and done, we eat for one of two reasons: hunger and appetite. These are not the same things. Hunger is the physical need for food. Your body releases certain chemicals and hormones when there is a need for energy and nutrition. Sometimes, hunger shows itself by bringing on feelings of weakness, lack of energy, headaches, or even lightheadedness. It is your body's way of telling you that the tank is getting low on fuel.

When it's all said and done, we eat for one of two reasons: hunger and appetite. These are not the same things.

Appetite is a psychological need for food that has little, if anything, to do with the physical need for nutrition. Any number of things can trigger appetite. Many people eat for comfort. For example, when Grand Mommy rewarded you for doing well in school with sweet potato pie, you learned to associate a feeling of success with pie. Each time you were hurt or crying and mommy baked you chocolate chip cookies, it reinforced the message that food could be used to heal all wounds, physical and emotional. As an adult, it's only natural that we try to reproduce those good feelings, and food lets us do so.

Unfortunately, the results are often self-destructive. Especially in cases like Lisa's. She, like a surprising number of women (men too, but this book is not about them), self-medicate. This means that they treat depression, anxiety, and, often, certain forms of psychological addiction with food. Hunger is no longer the trigger to eating. The triggers are emotional and psychological needs. So you can see how traditional "dieting" can place you on a yo-yo. The weight comes off, but what prompted the appetite—hurt, anger, pain, loss of control, and maybe even boredom—is still there. Unless, of course, you confront those issues and put them to rest once and for all.

Anorexia and Bulimia

No conversation about weight disorders would be complete without a mention of two very serious and often deadly diseases: anorexia nervosa and bulimia. You probably have a strange look on your face because this is a book about obesity, not about skinny people. But eating disorders are a spectrum. Morbid obesity is on one end, and anorexia and bulimia are on the other. All three conditions are frequently the outward display of depression and other psychiatric disorders.

Anorexia (the full name is "anorexia nervosa") is at the very extreme end of the eating disorder spectrum. When most of us think of anorexia, images of Hollywood actresses with extra-large heads placed atop necks the size of a straw come to mind. But although it is often the subject of jokes and derision, anorexia is actually a very serious disease. It is defined as both an eating disorder and a mental illness.

This "self-imposed starvation" is the result of a grossly distorted body image. People suffering from anorexia see themselves as fat, morbidly obese, even when they are, in fact, malnourished and underweight. Typically, those with anorexia are 25 percent or more below their normal weight. Starvation is the main mechanism anorexics use to decrease their body weight, but excessive exercise is used as well—many anorexics exercise five or six hours a day. The end result of anorexia can be death, which occurs because of heart rhythm abnormalities, dehydration, and congestive heart failure. So this is serious stuff.

The cause of anorexia is unknown, although there are several theories. There is most likely a biological predisposition to anorexia involving brain chemistry and the way you happen to be wired. Most people with anorexia have at least one family member who suffers from a psychiatric illness such as depression or obsessive-compulsive disorder. But although your genes may be involved, social attitudes that equate beauty with thinness also play a major role. In fact, anorexia is extremely rare in cultures and parts of the world where food is scarce and larger body sizes are considered signs of wealth and affluence.

Anorexia is closely linked with another eating disorder called "bulimia." People who have bulimia "binge and purge" in order to achieve weight loss. Specifically, bulimics have frequent "binges" where they eat great amounts of food in a short period of time (say, two hours) and feel that they lack control during the binging. The binge is then followed by the "purge," which is an attempt to get rid of all the food. People do this by forcing themselves to vomit (picture the finger down the throat). Purging is also done in other ways, such as over-use of laxatives and the misuse of diuretics.

Many of you may have attempted various forms of purging in your quest for quick weight loss. Does this make you bulimic? Not necessarily. The official definition of bulimia requires other characteristics and a certain amount of frequency. But you can see why bulimia fits somewhere in the middle of the spectrum. Especially because most bulimics are not terribly underweight. In fact, most are normal weight or slightly overweight. It goes to show that body size is not a good way to spot a bulimic (or anyone with an eating disorder).

Lurking in the background of eating disorders, whether the disorder is obesity, anorexia, bulimia, alone or in combination, we usually find serious emotional and psychological issues. Depression, anxiety, and abuse of various kinds are frequent flyers in the lives of those who are in a battle with their weight. Which comes first is hard to say. Was it the weight disorder that caused the depressed mood? Or is food (or deprivation of food) the "medication" that some use to treat the sadness? The bottom line is that issues of weight and of how we think about our bodies are complicated, and they can't be split apart.

Hey, it's Teri again, reaching for the tissue. When I heard Lisa's story, I was speechless. In fact, I cried. For that moment I knew what Lisa's suffering was because I shared it in my heart. But after the tears I realized that many of us—most of us, if we're honest—are only a biscuit or a personal tragedy away from being like Lisa. In fact, mentally we are Lisa, though probably with a little less body weight.

Some of you who have read thus far have probably thought, "I'm not that big, this doesn't apply to me." Or, "I'm not anorexic, bulimic, addicted, or clinically depressed," and you probably aren't. But think back to what Stacy said earlier about the differences between hunger and appetite. For most of us, our appetites rule our lives by determining our choices and, ultimately, how we act and react with our surroundings.

For a long time I thought I ate simply because I liked food. I do like food, and I love the entire food experience—the tastes, textures, flavors, and atmosphere. But I've also realized that I use food as a crutch. Law school was a particularly stressful time for me. I had a job and was going to school and working during the day—then studying into the wee hours of the night. Late-night snacking and heavy meals were the norm. I didn't bargain on the extra pounds that would come from the snacks, but they came.

Still, I thought everything was fine until a particularly nasty argument with my then-boyfriend changed my mind. During the argument, my boyfriend brought my weight into the "discussion," and I was crushed. Crushed and craving a cheeseburger.

He and I had lots of arguments during that time. He'd make comments about my weight, and then we'd argue. Sometimes I brought the subject up, and we'd argue some more. Each time, the result was that my feelings would be hurt and I'd crave a particular food. And eating would make me feel better.

My self-esteem is generally pretty high, as Stacy keeps telling you, but during these years I lost my self-esteem. I felt terrible about myself. I ate, I gained weight, I felt worse, and I ate more. I was on a roller coaster with no way to get off.

Sound familiar?

Don't get me wrong—I've never been one to share my difficulties with the world. So, with the exception of a few very close friends, most people thought I had a pretty perfect life and that I was ridiculously happy. For a long time the act was so good that even I was convinced. But my weight gain belied my smile. Something inside was broken, and until it was fixed, I was stuck.

Fast-forward five years.

Five years later, everything had changed. I was single and happy and had the benefit of hindsight.

But it didn't happen overnight. In order to get to this good emotional place, first I had to reflect deeply on how I'd gotten into the bad place. What I figured out was that for a long time, even after the relationship ended, I saw myself through my ex-boyfriend's eyes. And what I saw was big, fat, and miserable.

But one morning I looked in the mirror and something was different. For the first time in years, I looked at myself through my own eyes and not his. And what I saw through my own eyes wasn't so bad. In fact, it was pretty good! Yeah, I can still stand to lose a few pounds. But my heart is big. So are my dreams.

For the first time in years, I saw myself differently and I really liked what I saw. And, lo and behold, when that happened, others began to see me differently too! Ironically, those others included even the ex-boyfriend—who is now one of my closest (platonic!) male friends. And once I knew that I was good enough just the way I was, that inspired me to be better. I then felt like I deserved the best that I could give myself and deserved to be the best person I could become.

Maybe it's cliché, but I'm telling you because I know. How you see yourself is what determines how you're seen in the world. And you are beautiful. Today. Know it, believe it, and I guarantee you the world will respond in kind.

That said, a "new" person in the mirror doesn't appear without a lot of work and prayer and support. It didn't for me. And it won't for you.

It all comes down to one thing: You have to fix your head first. Aside from loving yourself, there are some specific tools that might be helpful if you're trying to get off of the "emotional eating roller coaster."

Keep a journal. By writing down when you eat and how you feel during that time, you will be able to see patterns. Examining those patterns may help you to understand what emotions and circumstances trigger your eating. Then you can replace bad, unhealthy habits with good ones (like taking a walk when you're sad instead of eating ice cream).

Eat a healthy diet. When your body is well nourished, it is better able to cope with emotional stresses. (See Chapter 10 for more on healthy diet.)

Exercise. Exercise makes your body and mind strong and relaxed. Limiting stress can also help to limit extreme emotional and hormonal swings, and in this way it also limit cravings and food binges

See a professional. Emotional eating is often attached to depression. Your doctor or a trained therapist can often work with you to figure out a counseling program (or in some instances, medications) that will help with underlying depression.

Meditate and pray.

When I talk about the connection between obesity and appetite, when I talk about the emotional ground of the weight problem, I'm not implying that all overweight women suffer from depression or any other psychiatric disorder. And I am not suggesting that every obese sister eats because she needs to fill some void or to escape from unpleasant memories or traumas. Many of us are overweight simply because we have poor eating habits and don't have the knowledge we need to correct them.

So the point isn't that you should look into yourself to find a disorder. What you need to do instead is evaluate your own specific food triggers. These will be different for each of you. One of the most effective ways to do that evaluation is by keeping a journal. For as long as it takes to identify your own food triggers, write down what you are feeling when you eat. Are you feeling sad, upset, frustrated, hurt, or perhaps just bored?

I've learned that my emotions are intimately attached to my appetite. So I know that during times when I'm feeling especially scared or emotional or vulnerable, I have to be careful not to "eat my emotions." When there's something to celebrate, I still cook, and when there's a victory, I still have drinks with friends. And on some of my bad days, I still want a cheeseburger!

Once you recognize and understand your major food triggers, be ready to take the next step. Focus on the how to break this cycle. The more clearly you know the issues that you face on the inside, the more ready you will be to take steps toward a healthy body and spirit.

I have to be honest with you. Looking at yourself—inside and out—without flinching is hard. Sometimes its ugly. And sometimes it's sad. But it is what you have to do in order to figure out what work needs to be done.

But on the other side, after the tears and the frustration and the heartache, there's a sparkly new mirror seen through your own brand-new set of eyes that will reflect to you a new, fresh perspective.

Take a peek. You're beautiful.

Part
Two

*Why
Obesity
Means
Health
Risks*

Chapter Four

Diabetes or, "A Little Bit of Suga'"

By now, after hearing Lisa's story and my sister's experiences, you've gotten the message that the battle with obesity is as much psychological as it is physical. But it is the physical manifestations of obesity that are responsible for the staggering levels of sickness and death seen in the African American community.

I know you've heard the following sayings before. You may have even used these yourself: "I've got sugar diabetes," or "I've got a little bit of sugar," or even "My blood's running a little sweet." I know you've heard the sayings before. You may have even used them. Those pretty words and phrases are commonly used to describe a not-so-pretty and potentially fatal disease that doctors call "diabetes mellitus." The casual way we talk about this disease shows how we, as a community, still fail to recognize the enormity of this killer. Contrary to commonly held beliefs, diabetes is very serious and very dangerous.

What Exactly Is Diabetes?

Here are some things you need to know to understand diabetes in relation to being overweight or obese. First, there are two separate types of diabetes. Although high blood sugar levels define both types, they have different causes and require different treatments.

The first kind is "Type I diabetes," which used to be known as "juvenile onset diabetes" because it is typically diagnosed in childhood. Type I diabetes has nothing to do with being overweight or with obesity. In fact, people with this type of diabetes are usually very thin.

The medical problem in Type I diabetes is the body's inability to make the insulin needed to control blood sugar levels. Insulin is the hormone that clears the sugar from the blood, and the pancreas is the organ that is mostly responsible for producing insulin, so in Type I diabetes, the pancreas stops making insulin at a very early age.

Type II diabetes has to do with obesity, and 2.3 million African Americans (or 11 percent) have been diagnosed with it, while countless others have it but are not aware of it.

I mention Type I diabetes only to distinguish it from the second form, Type II. Type II diabetes does have to do with obesity, and 2.3 million African Americans (or 11 percent) have been diagnosed with it, while countless others have it but are not aware of it.

And what about this statistic: One in four black women over the age of fifty-five suffers from Type II diabetes! This means that if you are in a room with eight or ten of your aunts, it's likely that at least two or three of them have the disease. (And they're probably the ones with the most food on their plates!) If several people in your family, now and in earlier generations, have had this illness, there are probably more family cases to come. And you could be one of them.

The main problem that leads to Type II diabetes is not the body's failure to produce insulin. Insulin is being made, but the body becomes resistant to the effects of the insulin. Why this happens is complicated. Sometimes it's because you inherited the trait from your parents, and at this time we can't do anything about that. However, genetics only predisposes a person to diabetes or any other illness. It takes other factors to turn that predisposition to actual disease. In the case of Type II diabetes, the critical factor is obesity.

What About Sugar?

Let's put to rest the myths that surround this disease. First and foremost, eating sugar does not cause diabetes. "But Doc, if the sugar in your body is too high, then it's obvious that eating too much sugar caused it, right?" Wrong! Fat, and the insulin resistance that follows from it, is the major cause of Type II diabetes.

Of course, if you eat too much sugar, it will eventually make you fat, but you can put on those extra pounds by eating just about anything in excess, including non-sugary foods such as burgers and fries. So how you choose to get fat is entirely up to you. When it comes down to it, how you gain weight is unimportant. If you are overweight, you are at risk for diabetes. And regarding the risk, sugar is not the issue. As we'll see later, the place on your body where you gain fat can increase your risk of developing diabetes, but for now, just understand that fat is the culprit. (For more about diet and wellness, see Chapter 10.)

Once you have been diagnosed with diabetes, the picture changes and it becomes essential that you set tight limits on your sugar intake. That means avoiding products like sweets and soda pop that contain a lot of processed, refined sugars. These are the kinds of sugars that cause blood sugar levels to increase quickly. We'll talk more later about the various kinds of sugars and the dietary management of diabetes. For now, just get it out of your head that sugar causes diabetes. Focus instead on the real cause, which is weight.

You might ask why doctors are so certain about this relationship between excess weight and diabetes. Certainly, medical science doesn't have all the answers, especially to problems as complex as diabetes. But the discovery that being fat meant you were more likely to get Type II diabetes first surfaced from simple observation. Researchers noted that the disease was uncommon in non-overweight populations. In Asian countries, where diets consisted mostly of fish and vegetables and the average person led an active, non-sedentary lifestyle, Type II diabetes was rare. The same held true for certain African populations as well.

At first, experts thought this variation in diabetes rates was because of ethnic differences. But that theory was dismissed when Asian populations began to adopt Western diets, which are high in fat and calories, and western lifestyles, which consist of watching the television or the computer while getting little physical activity in between. So with the spreading global popularity of fast food came the global epidemic of obesity and diabetes. Once the connection was understood, further research disclosed the relationship between excess body fat and the resistance to insulin.

Diabetes is uncommon in people with a BMI (body mass index) below 25. The trouble is that obesity rates, especially among African Americans, keep soaring. We are getting fatter at younger and younger ages. Diseases such as Type II diabetes, which used to be unheard of in children, are now becoming epidemic, and the major causes are the increasing weight and poor physical health of our youth. In fact, Type II diabetes was once known as "Adult Onset Diabetes," but that term can no longer be used because kids as young as twelve are showing up in the doctor's offices for treatment.

All right . . . this is all very interesting, and even alarming, but I don't see how it applies to me. I know (and you probably do, too) quite a few people who have diabetes and are overweight, and they sit on the couch and keep right on eating sweet potato pie. They don't look sick. They don't feel bad, and they're not in the hospital. And they keep eating sugar.

And now you tell me that sugar doesn't have anything to do with the causes of diabetes.

So, after all of this, I'm inclined to look at this entire chapter and think "So what?"

This is going to take a bit more explaining for me.

If diabetes isn't caused by sugar, why are there so many references to sugar?

If I get diabetes, what's the worst that can happen?

If I have diabetes, will I have to go on medication?

And, most importantly, if I have or get diabetes, can I still eat sweet potato pie?

That's my sister. Leave it to her to boil her entire medical health down to whether or not she can eat sweet potato pie. (And believe me, my sister can eat some sweet potato pie!) But this is serious business, so let's see if I can explain a little further—and I'll even answer her most important question first.

While it's a misconception that sugar causes diabetes, sugar remains an important player in the diabetes dynamic. When a person is insulin-resistant—that is, when they're diabetic—the body can't metabolize and process sugar. This means that any sugar taken into the body—by drinking sweet drinks or eating sweet potato pie—stays in the bloodstream. And sugar left in the bloodstream is dangerous. It causes damage to internal organs that you can't immediately reverse.

So if you have uncontrolled diabetes, that sweet potato pie is like a time bomb.

Once the diabetes is controlled (and we'll talk about control of diabetes later), very small amounts of processed sugar in an otherwise healthy lifestyle may be possible for some. But for most diabetics, sweets should become, and remain, a thing of the past. For many of you, that may be reason enough to get a hold of your weight and work to prevent diabetes in the first place!

Another myth about diabetes is reflected in the phrase "having a little bit of sugar." We hear that a lot, as if diabetes were a kind of joke, but the truth is that there is nothing funny or cute about this disease. Diabetes is serious business: It can and will destroy nearly every organ in the body if it's not treated aggressively.

True, people with diabetes (perhaps including yourself) can look pretty darn fine. But that's just on the outside. Now, you're about to learn the truth about what diabetes does to your insides.

Diabetes and the Heart

First, there's the heart. Diabetes dramatically increases the risk for circulatory and heart diseases like hypertension and heart attacks. Diabetes also causes these diseases to occur at an earlier age, and it increases the chance of dying from heart disease once you have been diagnosed. And for women, the natural protection against heart disease that estrogen affords us before menopause is eliminated if you have diabetes. The fact is, heart disease is the leading cause of death in people with diabetes.

Diabetes dramatically increases the risk for circulatory and heart diseases like hypertension and heart attacks.

There's a lot we don't know about why having high sugar levels is dangerous to the heart, but here, in a nutshell, is what we do know. High blood sugar levels are not the only abnormality in diabetes. The sugar levels also lead to numerous other changes, and these changes cause very bad things to happen in the blood vessels throughout the body, especially in the heart. They cause the heart vessels to function poorly and become more prone to getting clogged up with cholesterol and fat, leading to heart attacks.

Insulin resistance, the key problem in Type II diabetes, also contributes to the development of high blood pressure and causes the body to make the deadly forms of cholesterol that lead to heart attacks. To make matters worse, people with diabetes often suffer from "silent heart attacks." This means that heart attacks occur without any obvious signs or symptoms, thereby delaying life-saving treatment and frequently resulting in death.

When you don't feel any pain in your chest, you don't know that something bad is happening with your heart, so you don't go to see the doctor or go to the emergency room.

Diabetes and the Kidneys

The heart is not the only organ affected by diabetes. Diabetes is the number-one cause of kidney failure and subsequent dialysis, especially in African Americans. Every sister reading this book knows someone who is on, or has been on, dialysis. You may even be that someone.

Most of us think of our kidneys when we go to the bathroom, but getting rid of water is not the only job the kidneys perform. The kidneys are also responsible for filtering the blood and allowing waste to be eliminated from the body. They also play a role in regulating blood pressure. When the kidneys no longer work properly, it is necessary to be placed on dialysis. Dialysis is the process whereby you are hooked up to a machine that does the kidney's job of filtering your blood.

High sugar alone will eventually destroy the kidneys, but high sugar and high blood pressure will ruin them even faster!

One way to prevent this devastating complication of kidney failure is to carefully control blood sugars and aggressively control blood pressure. High sugar alone will eventually destroy the kidneys, but high sugar and high blood pressure will ruin them even faster!

Protein that's found in the urine (also called "microalbumin") is the earliest sign that there has been damage to the kidneys. This is a warning, and it needs to be aggressively treated to prevent the dialysis machine from becoming a part of your future

Diabetes and Blindness

Thought we were finished with the complications of diabetes? Not yet! Diabetes is the number-one cause of blindness in this country. In addition, diabetes is the number-one cause of non-traumatic amputations (meaning amputations not due to car accidents, etc). Just as the vessels in the heart get clogged and destroyed, so, too, can the vessels in the legs. When the feet and legs don't get adequate blood flow, they are more prone to ulcers and infections and in the end this leads to dead tissue. Once that destruction of tissue has gone far enough, there is no other alternative but to amputate. If you thought your feet were hurting now, try having them cut off!

As long as this list is, it's incomplete, because the effects of diabetes can be seen in just about every organ in the body. An entire book could be devoted exclusively to the complications of diabetes. However, our goal is to give you the information you need to know in order to make intelligent, educated decisions about your lifestyle choices. Diabetes, like many life-threatening illnesses in our community, is treatable and most importantly, *preventable*. But to prevent it, you must start by making certain changes.

So How Do You Know?

Could you possibly be sitting on the couch, reading this book, munching on a bag of salt and vinegar potato chips, and be suffering from diabetes and not even know it? If you are overweight or obese, there's a good chance that this is exactly what is happening. Unless diabetes has progressed to the point where your blood sugar levels are extremely high, it causes few, if any, symptoms. When there are signs, they can be rather vague, like blurred vision, fatigue, being very thirsty, and urinating a lot more than usual. Occasionally, your first sign can be a complication of diabetes, like foot ulcers or infections. For women, frequent vaginal yeast infections can also be a sign of undiagnosed diabetes.

Testing for Diabetes

The best way to know if you have diabetes is by seeing your doctor. The most commonly used screening test for diabetes is the "fasting blood sugar test." This is a blood test that is taken when you have an empty stomach, so your doctor will instruct you not to eat during the eight hours before the test.

Normal fasting blood sugar levels are between 70 and 110. A number greater than 126 is considered in the diabetic range. What if you fall somewhere between 110 and 126, or if your level is only slightly off? Think you're in the clear? Wrong! You may have "glucose intolerance," which translates into pre-diabetes. Glucose intolerance, just like full-blown diabetes, is associated with being overweight. And just like diabetes, it must be treated aggressively. Usually, if any abnormalities show up in the blood sugar test, you'll need further tests in order to pinpoint the diagnosis.

An even better test your doctor can do to determine if you are diabetic is a "glycosylated hemoglobin test" (also called the "hemoglobin A1c test"). This test gives your doctor the opportunity to see what your blood sugar has averaged over the past several months. This is a better indicator than a sugar level taken at just one brief moment in time, because your blood sugar fluctuates throughout the day depending on when and what you eat. The glycosylated hemoglobin test results are given as a percentage: less than 6 percent is considered normal.

This test is also used to monitor diabetes in patients who have already been diagnosed, and to determine if they are under optimal control. If you are diabetic, you must know your hemoglobin A1c level. If your level is more than 7 percent, your diabetes is not under optimal control, and you should discuss further treatment options with your doctor. If your doctor is not willing to make changes in the treatment, find another doctor! People with levels higher than 7 percent (and newer studies are saying the optimal level is 6.5 percent) are more likely to have all those potentially fatal complications of diabetes like heart attacks, amputations, strokes, kidney failure, and blindness.

The Good News: Treatment Options

Yes, diabetes is scary. But not everyone who has the disease ends up on a dialysis machine, or blind, or crippled with a heart

---

Diabetics can prevent complications by carefully controlling blood sugar levels and by monitoring and treating high blood pressure and cholesterol. To control the blood sugar levels, people with Type II diabetes have many treatment options.

---

attack. Diabetics can prevent complications by carefully controlling blood sugar levels and by monitoring and treating high blood pressure and cholesterol. To control the blood sugar levels, people with Type II diabetes have many treatment options.

Some people with Type II diabetes must be on insulin, either alone or in combination with other drugs (today, unlike in the past, there are newer kinds of insulin that are taken only once a day). There are also several new and exciting medications that are being used to control diabetes. These drugs are revolutionary because they actually attack the cause of Type II diabetes, which is insulin resistance.

There is also an older family of drugs you may have heard of, such as glyburide and glypizide. What these drugs do is to force your body to release more insulin from the pancreas (the pancreas is the organ that makes insulin). These are still used to treat diabetes, but they are more effective when combined with the newer medications that specifically address the body's inability to use the insulin that is already produced.

There are two classes of newer drugs. The first class is called "thioglidizones" (drugs such as Actos® or Avandia®). The second class of drugs is called "biguanides" and include the drug metformin (the trade name is Glucophage®). Get out a sheet of paper and write these names down. If you have been diagnosed with diabetes and you are not on one or both of these medications, immediately ask your doctor why. There may be a good reason. Not all people are candidates for these drugs (such as those with advanced liver or kidney disease). Or there may not be a good reason, and perhaps you should consider finding another physician.

The ugly reality is that African Americans continue to get the short end of the stick when it comes to health care, and we are often denied potentially lifesaving treatments simply because we are uninformed and don't have the knowledge to "speak up." But all of that is about to change. In fact, it just did in the time it took to read this page. See, knowledge is a beautiful thing!

Drugs are good and you shouldn't be afraid of them. They are often necessary in order to control blood sugar levels effectively. But what if I told you that there might be a way to treat your diabetes without drugs?

Remember that the major cause of Type II diabetes is *fat* and that diabetes is relatively uncommon in people with a BMI of 25 or less. So what would happen if an overweight person were diagnosed with diabetes, but then changed her diet and exercise habits to lose the weight? Could this person then be off medications for good? Yes, Yes, Yes! This scenario is what I like to call the "diabetes success story." And it does happen. Weight loss, exercise, and changes in eating habits are *critical* in the treatment and management of diabetes.

True, there are cases where people get down to their goal weight and change their eating habits but still must stay on medications. But it is almost always possible to reduce the number of medicines needed and/or to decrease the dose. I don't know about you, but most of us would prefer taking one or two pills a day instead of four pills plus an insulin injection.

This information is scary, and it's all new to me (and probably to a lot of people), so I guess I'm learning. But now that we have the information, what are we supposed to do with it?

This information isn't meant to scare you. Having the right

kind of knowledge, in the long run, is much less scary than living in ignorance. When it comes to your health, the best offense is a good defense. For those of you who do not have diabetes, the key is to do everything possible to prevent this life-threatening illness. This applies to you, and to the children in your homes and in your communities.

The way to take the offensive is by fighting against obesity and encouraging those you love and care for to do the same. Yes, exercise is hard, as can be switching to a healthy diet. Losing weight is hard. Just staying out of the fast food drive-thru can be damn hard. But dialysis is even harder. Giving yourself insulin injections and checking your blood sugar three times a day is harder. Recovering from strokes and heart attacks is hard and sometimes even impossible. So while taking good care of yourself and your loved ones may mean some hard choices, the choices are nothing compared to cost of *not* taking care of yourself.

While this book is about educating yourself in order to avoid a dangerous disease, it is also about empowerment. It's about taking control of your health and responsibility for your body. You might even find that once you've don't that, a lot of other goals you thought impossible begin to look much more achievable.

So take the first step by walking into your physician's office armed with information. That's the only way you can know if your treatment is appropriate, if your doctor is competent, and if you are putting your health at risk without even knowing it.

With that in mind, here are some key points to discuss with your doctor. Write them down, and take them on your next trip to your health professional.

Diabetes Questions to Ask Your Doctor

1. Ask your doctor what your BMI (body mass index) is, and what your optimal weight is and how to get there. (Don't be content with "You need to lose weight." Work out a reasonable diet and exercise plan, preferably in writing.)

2. Ask for a fasting blood sugar test. If the results are higher than 126, ask for a hemoglobin A1c test. If the results are between 110 and 126, demand more testing. You may be glucose intolerant or have full-blown diabetes. In both cases, you must be treated.

3. If you have been diagnosed with diabetes, know your hemoglobin A1c level. If it is greater than 6.8 percent to 7 percent, discuss treatment options with your doctor.

4. Demand a fasting cholesterol test, and discuss medications and dietary changes needed if the numbers are high (more on these numbers later).

5. Know your blood pressure goals (important for everyone, but extremely important if you are diabetic). Your top number should be around 120, your bottom number around 70. If you are not at this goal, additional treatment is needed.

6. If you have diabetes, ask for a urine test to see if there is protein called "microalbumin" present. If there is, discuss the use of medications (called "ACE Inhibitors" or ARBs) to stop the progression of kidney disease. (More on these drugs later.)

7. If you have diabetes, you must have an eye exam by an eye doctor every year.

8. Because of the serious risk of foot infections and ulcers, see a podiatrist (that's a fancy word for a foot doctor) every year and check your feet for calluses and sores each day.

Remember, what it finally comes down to is that you are in control. Not your mom or dad, not your spouse, and not your doctor. It's your body, your life, and your health.

Chapter Five

Heart Disease or, "Behind the Breast ™"[3]

I remember my first boyfriend. I was in seventh grade at Oliver Wendell Holmes Middle School, and he was in eighth grade. He was cute, and quiet and popular. He ran track, had these "bow-legs" that equated with "fine" in Texas in the '80s, and we talked on the phone for hours at a time. I was a staple at his track meets. And I remember that we held hands, and we kissed. A lot.

At some point, we broke up. Now, after all these years, I can't remember exactly when or why. But what I do remember is that my young heart was absolutely broken.

Needless to say, even though that was the first time, it certainly wasn't the last time my heart was broken. I think heartbreak is somehow part of our lives as women. And as a woman, the only time I really even think about my heart is when it hurts—or when it breaks. And I don't think I'm the exception.

---

3. Behind the Breast.™ Behind the Breast™ is a registered trademark and non-profit organization founded by Dr. Stacy Mitchell for the education and prevention of heart disease in women.

Well, this time my sister got it right: As women, we generally don't think of our hearts until they get broken. This is unfortunate, considering that heart disease, in the form of high blood pressure and heart attacks, is the leading cause of death in women. In fact, heart disease in women causes more deaths each year than breast cancer, colon cancer, cervical cancer, lung cancer, AIDS, car accidents, suicides, and homicides combined.

Let me make sure you heard me. Heart disease in women causes more deaths each year than breast cancer, colon cancer, cervical cancer, lung cancer, AIDS, car accidents, suicides and homicides combined!

Add to that the fact that black women are diagnosed much later in the disease process, and that, once we are diagnosed, we die sooner than women and men of other ethnic groups. Now you can see why we should all be thinking of our hearts—not just in the context of heartbreak but also in the context of heart disease.

The main reason I have dedicated a large portion of my medical practice to women and heart disease is that heart disease gives us so many opportunities for prevention. Many of the causes of heart problems are directly related to our own self-destructive behaviors. I often joke with my patients and say that if black people stopped smoking and eating so much, I'd be out of business! It always gets a laugh, but it isn't funny.

Heart disease in women causes more deaths each year than breast cancer, colon cancer, cervical cancer, lung cancer, AIDS, car accidents, suicides and homicides combined!

Along with smoking, obesity is one of the major lifestyle choices that lead to cardiovascular disease. The term cardiovascular disease describes illnesses that affect the heart and the large vessels in the body that lead to the heart. The main types of cardiovascular disease are hypertension (also known as "high blood pressure") and heart attacks. There are other types, such as disease of the arteries in the legs (called "peripheral vascular disease"), but I'll focus on hypertension and heart attacks because they kill the most within the black community (more than crack or guns ever have or ever will!).

> *Along with smoking, obesity is one of the major lifestyle choices that lead to cardiovascular disease.*

Oh, the PRESSURE!

What exactly is hypertension, and why do we care?

There are two types of hypertension: "secondary" and "essential" (also called "primary"). Secondary hypertension simply means that some underlying disease is the cause. In such cases, treatment of that illness will usually resolve the high blood pressure. Examples of secondary hypertension include diseases of the adrenal glands (Cushing's disease), or blockage of the arteries of the kidneys. Medications such as birth control pills or steroids can also cause or contribute to secondary hypertension. In all of these cases, if you treat the disease or stop the drug, the high blood pressure goes down. Secondary hypertension makes up a very small part of all cases—less than 5 percent.

The vast majority of African Americans have "essential" hypertension, which means no underlying illness is the cause. So from now on, in discussing blood pressure we will be talking about essential hypertension only.

High blood pressure happens when the small arteries and vessels that transport blood throughout the body begin to get stiff. Because of this stiffness, blood has to flow at higher pressure in order to force its way through the vessels and to the rest of the body. The higher pressure eventually damages and weakens the arteries. This means that the heart (which pumps the blood) must work even harder to force blood through these smaller, stiffer vessels. Just as your arms get bigger when you lift weights, your heart gets bigger when it is forced to work harder than it should.

High blood pressure happens when the small arteries and vessels that transport blood throughout the body begin to get stiff.

But what is good for your biceps is very bad for your heart, and this enlargement of the heart because of increased blood pressure is the first step along the road that will end in heart failure.

When your doctor or health professional takes your blood pressure, two numbers are recorded.

The top number is the systolic pressure. It is the pressure your heart generates each time it contracts to pump blood.

The bottom number is the diastolic pressure. It is the pressure that your arteries are under when the heart relaxes in between each beat.

So what is "normal" blood pressure? Good question, but the answer is a bit more complicated than you might think. In fact, I don't use the term "normal" in describing blood pressure. The group you are a part of determines "normal," and if that group consists of black women, then "normal" is actually dangerously high! I prefer to use the term "optimal."

Optimal pressure for someone with no other serious illnesses (like diabetes) is a systolic reading (top number) of less than 130, and a diastolic reading (bottom number) of less than 85. However, "optimal" blood pressure is different if you have diabetes, kidney disease, or heart disease (like heart attacks or heart failure). In these cases, your blood pressure goal is a top number less than 120 and a bottom number less than 80. For most of you, these numbers are surprising, because they seem so incredibly low. Believe me, I have received countless "emergency" calls from patients who are frantic that their pressure is too low at 115/70, and they want to know if they should stop their medicine. I simply congratulate them on finally achieving an optimal pressure and pat myself on the back.

A Peek into the Future

Just about every black person I know over the age of forty-five has high blood pressure. I'll bet everybody over forty-five that you know has high blood pressure, too! To prove my point, I dare you to go to the medicine cabinet of anyone over forty-five and peek in. I guarantee you will find "pressure pills." This, to me, leads to a seemingly logical question: If everybody has it, how bad can it be?

People usually don't take high blood pressure very seriously, but as African Americans, we definitely should. One out of three black adults has high blood pressure, and, as a group, we are more than twice as likely to develop high blood pressure in our lifetimes than white Americans. We are also more likely to suffer from, and die from, the complications of high blood pressure.

Which brings us to the all-important question: "What happens if blood pressure is not controlled?" The answer to this question is scarier than Halloween.

First, let's start with the dangers that aren't so obvious, the things you may not expect.

Controlling Your Blood Pressure

When your blood pressure is not controlled, as it should be, many parts of the body can suffer serious damage. For an example, hypertension is the second leading cause of kidney failure in this country (the number-one cause is diabetes). Similar to the way that high pressure destroys the heart, that same pressure works to destroy the kidneys.

Another very serious result of poorly controlled blood pressure, one that could change your life forever, is stroke. Strokes happen when there is a blocked or ruptured blood vessel in the brain. When that happens, the part of the brain that receives blood and oxygen from the blocked or ruptured vessel dies.

The brain is like a detailed map. There is a very specific part of the brain that controls movement of your right leg, or your ability to talk. Other parts of the brain control the muscles that allow you to swallow or smile, and even the muscles that allow you to breathe. When a stroke occurs, certain body functions can be wiped out, depending on the area of the brain where the blockage or bleeding occurred.

If you are African American, chances are you or someone in your family has suffered a stroke, and you know that the results can be devastating and even fatal. Often, people who have had strokes lose the ability to move parts of their bodies. The resulting paralysis causes overwhelming difficulties—not only for the person who had the stroke but also for the family and friends who must now care for her and pay for her care.

Sometimes, God gives you a warning, such as a "mini stroke." This is when you have the symptoms of a stroke but those symptoms disappear in about an hour or less. These mini strokes don't cause major damage but are a sign that you are at risk of having a full-blown stroke next time. If you ever have a mini stroke, it is urgently important that you take it very seriously.

High blood pressure is the number-one cause of strokes. There are other causes, such as blood clots being thrown from the heart, but high blood pressure is by far the most common cause. The high pressures that are so destructive for the heart vessels also weaken the vessels in and surrounding the brain, making them more likely to burst or to become clogged.

Strokes are not the only things that can go wrong in your head when blood pressure remains high and out of control. Hypertension is a common cause of blindness in the African American population. The reasons are the same for the eyes as they are for the heart and the brain. The arteries in the eyes are sensitive and are easily damaged by the increased pressures. Eventually, this damage can result in loss of vision.

Watch Your Heart

Now we come to the most common and widely known result of high blood pressure—damage to the heart. Remember that when the heart has to pump blood through stiff, small arteries, it's getting quite a workout. And the heart is a muscle, so when it is worked extra hard, it gets bigger. This is not good. The process of the heart enlarging in medical terms is called "left ventricular hypertrophy," and it is a sign of long-standing, poorly controlled blood pressure.

There are two widely used tests that your doctor can do to see if you have this complication. The first is an electrocardiogram, or EKG. This test is very simple (and painless) and is done in a few minutes in the doctor's office. The second test is more effective in detecting ventricular hypertrophy, and is called an echocardiogram. The echocardiogram is similar to the ultrasound used to look at babies in the womb. It is a bit more expensive than an EKG, but it gives an actual, real-time picture of the heart. It, too, is painless.

You may be thinking, "Yeah, yeah, so my heart is a little big and stiff. What of it?" Well, hypertrophy and stiffness of the heart inevitably leads to the heart not being able to pump blood effectively, and congestive heart failure is the likely outcome. Congestive heart failure occurs when the heart no longer works as it should and fluid builds up in various parts of the body, especially the lungs (inhibiting your ability to breath), legs (making your shoes not fit), and abdomen. At some point, the heart weakens to a point where it can no longer sustain life, and this condition becomes fatal.

If your EKG or echocardiogram shows evidence of ventricular hypertrophy, this means you are at a much greater risk of death due to heart disease, and you *must* aggressively control your blood pressure (as well as other things, like cholesterol and blood sugar).

High blood pressure can also dramatically increase the risk of heart attacks. The high pressure in the arteries and vessels of the heart damages the inside lining of those arteries. When the arteries are damaged, it makes them more vulnerable to arteriosclerosis and clogging of the arteries, leading to heart attacks (more on heart attacks soon). The result is dead heart muscle, and if enough heart muscle is damaged, the heart can no longer sustain life—in other words, you die.

But I Feel Great

Can you tell if you have high blood pressure without having your pressure checked? No! Is it possible to be walking around for many years, thinking everything is fine, when your high blood pressure is actually at work destroying several organs in your body? Yep! That is why high blood pressure is often called the "silent killer." Hypertension usually has no symptoms until a complication (kidney failure, stroke, heart failure, or heart attack) occurs. Then the symptoms are related to the complication, but not usually to the high blood pressure itself. Some people report knowing their pressure is high because of headaches or blurry vision. Others say they feel more tired. As you can see, these possible symptoms are very vague, and most of us have experienced headaches and fatigue without having high blood pressure. That is why hypertension is so dangerous. It sneaks up on you, and often there are no warning signs until something catastrophic happens.

That is why hypertension is so dangerous. It sneaks up on you, and often there are no warning signs until something catastrophic happens.

So What Causes It?

By now, you probably realize just how dangerous high blood pressure is, and how it can cause devastating things to happen—even death. But what exactly causes these horrible changes that occur in the arteries and make them damaged and stiff, leading ultimately to high blood pressure? No one can describe completely why people get high blood pressure, but there is a lot we *do* know.

Genetics, or the traits you inherit from your parents, has a part in determining whether you are predisposed to high blood pressure. You can't choose your parents, so I won't spend much time talking about it. But always remember, just as with diabetes, a predisposition does not equal disease. It only means that very close attention must be paid to controlling the other factors that put you at risk.

Dietary factors such as diets that are high in salt or low in potassium and calcium can contribute to increased blood pressure. This is especially true in African American populations. Lack of physical activity and excessive amounts of alcohol are recognized as causes of hypertension as well. But because we're concentrating on obesity, you have probably correctly guessed what the major factor is in developing high blood pressure. That's right. FAT.

Being overweight or obese has profound effects on blood pressure. The reasons are somewhat complicated (and maybe even a bit boring to most), but you can simply use your common sense to figure out the basic problem. Just mentally picture a normal heart inside an average-sized body. In women, the heart weighs about nine ounces (which is a little more than half a pound). Remember that its job is to pump blood to every part of the body, from the top of the head, to the tip of the toes. The heart has a formidable job because it pumps about 2000 gallons of blood each day! Can you picture it? Good.

Now picture that same nine-ounce heart placed inside a body that is a hundred pounds heavier, attempting to pump 2,000 gallons of blood throughout this body. Can you picture it? (If not, perhaps you can imagine the engine from a Ford Escort placed inside a Cadillac truck. In either case, the poor engine's days are numbered!)

That excessive weight is a mechanical burden on the heart. But that's only one problem. Another is that the greater number of fat cells also produces an increased number of hormones such as insulin. Remember hearing the term insulin resistance in the diabetes section? Well, when fat cells make lots of insulin, your body can't clear it all from the blood (which is the job of the liver) so the cells of the body become insulin-resistant. This resistance to insulin plays a key role in developing high blood pressure (in addition to diabetes and maybe even cancer).

But maybe we are getting too "technical." My dear sister Teri will probably jump in pretty soon, complaining as usual (she thinks that medical information should be strictly on a "need to know" basis). And you may feel this way, too, so to recap:

Fat = Hypertension = BAD!

I hope this satisfies Teri's need for simplicity. And I hope it gets the message across. Let's move on.

Yes, blood pressure goes up as weight goes up, no way around it. But there is some good news in all this. For one, in people who are overweight or obese, even a small amount of weight loss (as little as 10 to 15 pounds) can have a marked effect on lowering blood pressure. So a little can go a long way. There is more good news. High blood pressure is easily diagnosed and easily treated, and even easily preventable. But if you have been diagnosed with hypertension, it takes some dedication, hard work, and education to stop all those bad things like kidney failure, heart failure, and strokes from being a part of your future. You already are on the road to educating yourself (you're reading this book), so now let's look at what exactly is involved in treating this "silent killer."

High blood pressure is easily diagnosed, easily treated, and even easily preventable.

What to Do

Hypertension is treated in four ways:

- Diet
- Exercise
- Weight loss, if needed
- Medications

Diet and exercise should *always* be part of the treatment plan. This may not be what you wanted to hear, but it is the truth. It may seem far easier just to take a pill or two each day than to watch what you eat, avoid fast food, and regularly exercise. But if your doctor has only used medicines to treat your blood pressure, then she is not doing her job. Medications are often needed, but in some cases the blood pressure can be controlled with the first two treatments. Even if you must stay on medication, it will work best if you are also watching what you eat and getting your exercise.

Some people have what is considered "mild" hypertension (meaning the top number is in the 140 range and the bottom number is in the 90 range), and do not have other illnesses like diabetes or kidney disease. For such cases, often the first treatment involves an exercise program and weight loss. Your weight loss diet program will be combined with a diet low in salt. Diets low in salt (also called "sodium") lower blood pressure even in people who do not have hypertension.

> *Diet and exercise should always be part of the treatment plan.*

So how much salt is too much? Let's put it this way: The average American diet includes 4,000 milligrams of salt a day. Our diets (meaning us black folk) probably have even higher amounts of salt. Salt is necessary for life and for your body to function normally, but the amount that is optimal for good health is around 2,500 milligrams. This is approximately one tablespoon of salt. You may think there is no way you put that much salt on your food every day. Well, you don't have to. It's already been done for you. Salt not only makes things taste good, but it is also a preservative, so it is found in large amounts in processed foods like chips, salad dressing, and many packaged foods. There's also a lot of salt in fast foods. Take, for example, a hamburger with cheese. There are 1,350 milligrams of salt in this one sandwich! If you add a medium order of fries (and when was the last time you ate a medium anything at a fast food restaurant?) that's another 300 milligrams. So in just one meal, you have consumed 1650 milligrams of salt. If you "super size" it, you are up to 2000 milligrams! And even things that don't taste salty have salt; for example, a vanilla shake will give you another

High-Salt Foods

Bacon

Baking powder

Baking soda

Beans (canned)

Bouillon (beef or chicken)

Bologna

Buttermilk (commercial)

Canned meats (beef stew,
   chili)

Canned soups

Canned vegetables

Cheese

Chitlins (pickled)

Fast foods

Frozen prepared foods

Hamburger

Ham hock

Hog maw (pickled)

Hot dogs

Instant grits

Instant oatmeal

Ketchup

Luncheon meats

Monosodium glutamate
   (MSG)

Mustard

Olives

Pickles (dill or onion)

Pig's feet (pickled)

Pizza

Pot pies

Potato chips

Pretzels

Salted nuts

Saltines

Sauerkraut

Sausage

Seasonings[*]

Self-rising flour or meal

Soda crackers

Soy sauce

Steak sauces

Tomato juice

TV dinners

* Garlic salt, seasoning salt, onion salt, allspice, MSG, teriyaki, lemon
  pepper, premixed seasonings for meat, poultry, and fish

300 milligrams. And all of this is before you ever reach for the salt shaker.

If you have high blood pressure, your salt intake should be even less than the 2,500 milligrams that people without high blood pressure should consume. You should aim for 2,000 milligrams of salt per day. The only way to hit that target is to become a master at reading the labels. The government requires that all food products have a label attached that gives the nutritional content of the food, including fat and cholesterol. But sometimes they try to trick you. Take, for instance, an individual bag of potato chips. The amount of salt, fat, and calories listed is per serving. Most people consider that single bag a serving, but that bag actually contains two and a half servings. At the top of the label, it will tell you how many servings are in the bag, but you have to look carefully. Stay tuned: there will be more on reading labels a bit later.

Lowering your salt level is an effective way of lowering your blood pressure. Exercise and physical activity are additional ways to do the life-saving job. To get your blood pressure down, you'll need forty-five minutes of aerobic activity, at least three to four times a week. (Aerobic activity is any activity that gets your heart rate up to a certain level—your target heart rate—and keeps it up there for at least twenty minutes.)

To figure out what your target heart rate is, take your age in years and subtract that from 220. This gives you your maximum heart rate. Your target heart rate is 60 percent to 80 percent of this number. Once you know your target heart rate, you then have to check your actual heart rate during exercise.

Please stop. My eyes are rolling back in my head. I feel like all of these numbers have put me AT my target heart rate! So let's take a break— if you can call it a break when a stressful subject comes up.

Stress is bad for your heart, just like too much salt intake and lack of exercise. Stress increases cortisol levels in the blood, which is thought to cause damage to your heart (and rumor has it, it may even contribute to weight gain!).

So when you're feeling stressed, try this:

Close your eyes and picture something tranquil. Take three long deep breaths. Can you feel your blood pressure going down? Good. Take another deep breath. Breathe. Get into the habit of doing this whenever you face a stressful situation.

Now, take a deep breath and we'll return to Stacy.

Teri is actually right to say that stress can contribute to high blood pressure, and she makes a good suggestion about how to manage stress. Here's another: exercise!

Before and after exercise sessions, whatever the exercise, take your pulse to make sure that your heart rate is within your target range. Your pulse can be most easily felt either at your neck or under the left breast, where your heart can be felt beating at its strongest, but you can also feel it on your wrist. (Many aerobic machines in gyms also check your heart rate automatically if you follow the instructions). During an exercise session, once your heart rate is up to where it needs to be, you must keep it there for at least twenty minutes.

Most of you reading this have probably realized that what you consider good exercise really isn't cuttin' it. That leisurely walk around the block or through the mall doesn't qualify as the type of exercise needed to lower blood pressure (or burn fat) effectively. Unless your doctor says that you shouldn't do aerobic exercise, you should. Working up to aerobic exercise may take a little time, but the results are worth it. All it takes is patience and determination.

As to the payoff, on average, low-salt diets and aerobic exercise alone can lower systolic pressure (the top number) by 12 points and the diastolic pressure (bottom number) by 5 points. So you can see how people with mild blood pressure can be treated without medicines. (If you have blood pressure in the higher range, or have other diseases, such as diabetes or other forms of heart disease, you will still need medicines.)

Many different types of medication effectively lower blood pressure. If one medicine is not effective, then your doctor must add a second drug, and sometimes even a third, fourth, or fifth drug.

Talking about each type of medication is beyond the scope of this book, but there are a few important things you should be aware of when it comes to high blood pressure medications. Write these down if you need to and discuss them with your doctor.

- First, if you have diabetes, or have had congestive heart failure, a history of heart attacks or heart disease, or kidney problems, and if your blood pressure is not at its optimal level, one of the types of medicines your doctor should consider putting you on is a class of drugs called "ACE inhibitors." ACE inhibitors are very effective at halting the progression of kidney disease and heart disease—especially in people with diabetes.
- Some people are allergic to ACE inhibitors, and in those cases, a doctor should consider using drugs called "Angiotensin receptor blockers" or ARBs, which are equally effective.
- Another type of blood pressure medicine called "beta-blockers" may be a good choice if you have ever had a heart attack, or if the reduced pumping function of your

heart is causing congestive heart failure. (Some people cannot use beta-blockers—namely, people with asthma or other forms of lung disease or with very low heart rates.)

Ask your doctor about these medicines. They may help significantly to prevent more heart attacks or the progression of heart failure.

If you do not have any of the above illnesses and just need to be treated for the high blood pressure alone, the important thing is to get the pressure down, using whatever medications do the trick. Sometimes this requires several medications, in addition to diet changes, exercise, and weight loss. All medications have some potential side effects, and blood pressure medicines are no exception. With most blood pressure drugs, the main side effects include fatigue, headaches, and dizziness. But after you've been on the medications for a few weeks, these symptoms usually clear up. So don't be one of those people who decide to stop taking their medicines because they don't like the side effects. Give the drugs a chance to do their work. Remind yourself that your life could be at stake.

For most people, blood pressure drugs cause only mild symptoms, if any. Often, symptoms people think are due to the

---

Don't be one of those people who decide to stop taking their medicines because they don't like the side effects. Give the drugs a chance to do their work. Remind yourself that your life could be at stake.

---

medicine are actually due to the body adjusting to a normal blood pressure. People may live with extremely high pressures for months, even years, before they are diagnosed and treated. The body gets used to these high pressures, so when the pressure is finally brought down, there may be a brief "adjustment period" and some mild fatigue or dizziness.

The important thing to remember is that the complications of high blood pressure, such as stroke, heart attack, and blindness, are always worse than mild side effects of blood pressure medicines. It may take some adjustment of your drug regimen, or trying different drugs, but whatever you do, don't stop your medications without discussing it with your doctor.

In my own experience, people hate to take medicines. They can be expensive, and it's hard to remember to take several drugs, several times a day. Yet millions of African American women have to do just that. A far better and surer way is to prevent high blood pressure by—you guessed it—preventing obesity and fighting the fat. So if you're overweight and haven't been diagnosed with high blood pressure, lose the weight and you may avoid medications completely. If you have already been diagnosed with high blood pressure, often, along with weight loss and diet changes, the number and dose of the medications can be reduced. Some people are able to come off of drugs completely.

A Heavy Heart

The other major type of cardiovascular disease that is strongly related to obesity is heart attack, known to doctors as "myocardial infarctions." A heart attack occurs when the arteries that supply blood and oxygen to the heart get blocked and the part of the heart that is supplied by that blocked artery dies. Coronary artery disease is the term used to describe this blockage of the arteries, while heart attack occurs when the blockage is complete and part of the heart dies. You can have coronary artery disease without having a heart attack; in fact many people do.

One way to understand coronary artery disease and heart attack is to think of a major highway that leads into a city. This highway is the only way for the people in the city to get supplies of food. Every day, truckloads of items are brought into the city. Everything is running smoothly until one day a truck jackknifes and blocks three of the five lanes of the highway. Although this is a serious problem, supplies can still get through to the city using the remaining two lanes of traffic. Of course, things are moving much more slowly, and the people in the city will be receiving fewer supplies because of the delay.

This scenario is like coronary artery disease. Substitute "highway" for "blood vessel" and "city" for "heart" and you start to see the picture. In the heart, instead of a jackknifed big rig, partial blockage is usually caused by a cholesterol plaque. Blood can still get through because the blockage is not complete, but the blood supply is definitely restricted. As long as "traffic" is light enough (for instance at 1 A.M.), the remaining two lanes of traffic may be enough to bring in the necessary items.

What would happen if the big rig jackknifed and blocked all the lanes of traffic? No food or supplies would get through to the city, and this means big trouble. If the blockage is not relieved quickly, the people of the city will starve and die because their food supply is cut off. The same occurs with heart muscle. If the cholesterol plaque is not removed as soon as possible, then heart muscle dies because of the lack of blood and oxygen. If a large portion of heart muscle dies, then the heart no longer pumps effectively, and heart failure, and eventually death, occurs. And the thing about heart attacks is that they don't discriminate. Under the right (or wrong) conditions, they can happen to anyone, anytime. Including you.

A few years ago, shortly after New Year's 2001, I got a message on my voicemail from my friend Lori. "Hey girl, this is Lori. Call me when you can." I knew she was planning to head out on a cruise. Lori's a travel agent and always going somewhere wonderful, and I figured she was calling to tell me all about the trip. But I was busy and didn't call her back.

A couple of days later, she called me again. This time she got me. And what she had to tell me was something I never would have guessed.

On New Year's Eve, forty-year-old Lori had a heart attack. Here's what she told me:

Lori and her loving husband, Vincent, had a New Year's Eve party. After the guests were gone and the kitchen was clean, Lori and Vincent went to bed. Not long after turning in, Lori had indigestion that felt like a burning in her chest. The possible indigestion didn't really surprise her, considering all of the food and champagne and celebrating they had done all night.

So Lori raised her hands over her head, hoping to burp and relieve some of the tightness. The discomfort did go away, but only for a little while. Not long after, she woke up feeling like she couldn't breathe. Her right arm was aching and she got up to go into the kitchen for some water. Lori never made it to the kitchen.

As she tried to get out of bed, Lori says her right arm suddenly felt like it was on fire. She had an overwhelming pain in her chest—"like an elephant standing on my breast" was how she described it. And as she fell to the floor, she couldn't catch her breath enough to call Vincent's name to wake him up. So she hit the side of the bed until he woke up and saw her lying on the floor. Vincent got Lori to the hospital, which was right up the street, and what the doctors told her when she arrived is something she never expected to hear: forty-year-old seemingly healthy Lori had suffered a major heart attack.

Women often do not have the "typical" symptoms of heart attacks—like chest pain that extends down the left arm. Sometimes, instead, we experience heartburn-type discomfort, as Lori did, or even just problems catching our breath. Women who are diabetic are especially likely to have "silent" heart attacks—meaning there are few symptoms or none at all. The best way to avoid a silent heart attack is to eliminate such major risks of heart disease as smoking and weight gain.

Because of "silent" heart attacks, for one third of all people, the first symptom of heart disease is sudden death. That's right, in 33 percent of cases, people walk around with no clue that they have a problem with blockage of the arteries, until they collapse, dead. This is not to say that they were not at risk for heart attacks. It means that the risk factors were not being addressed.

Lori was lucky. She got to the hospital quickly and doctors there acted fast.

How do you know if you have blockage of the arteries or if you have suffered, or are suffering, a heart attack? First, you must ask yourself and your doctor if you are at risk for this disease. If you are fat, then the answer is "yes." If you smoke, have a family history of heart problems, have high blood pressure or diabetes, again the answer is "yes." Age is also a factor, and, as a woman, your chances of having this form of heart disease increases greatly after menopause.

In cases where there are symptoms of blocked arteries, the most typical symptom is angina. Angina simply means chest pain. Chest pain occurs when the heart is not getting enough blood and oxygen. Often, this pain will happen when you are exerting yourself, as in walking or going up stairs. With activity, your heart requires more blood and oxygen. But if your arteries are partially blocked, they are not able to deliver the increased supply of blood to your heart muscle that the exertion demands. That's when you get pain in your chest. (Think of rush-hour traffic trying to squeeze through one lane of the highway.)

Usually, if the activity (like walking or climbing stairs) is stopped, the demand for blood and oxygen decreases and the pain goes away. However, if the arteries are extremely blocked, then not enough blood gets to your heart muscles even when you are sitting still at rest. This stage is very dangerous and leads to heart attacks, which occur when the heart muscle actually dies.

After a few days, Lori was stabilized and her questions began. Why did this happen to her? How did it happen? How does she keep it from happening again? Is there anything she could have done to prevent it?

Turns out, the things that Lori thought were "normal" were the things that made her prone to a heart attack. Lori had mildly high blood pressure; she was overweight, ate a bad diet, and didn't get much exercise.

The causes of heart attacks and coronary artery disease are much like the causes of just about every other type of disease. There are risk factors, like genetics, that we can do nothing about. If you have parents who had heart attacks, especially if they began to experience heart problems before the age of fifty, you are much more at risk for having blockage of the arteries. But this book is about taking responsibility for those things we can control, and coronary artery disease and heart attacks are among the most preventable diseases.

Other than genetics, most of the conditions that contribute to this form of heart disease are directly associated with obesity. But one habit not related to obesity that poses a huge risk to your heart and to just about every other part of your body as well is smoking. Cigarette smoking is the single most destructive thing you can do to your health. The chemicals found in tobacco smoke quickly act to destroy the vessels in the heart and throughout the body, and they also cause many types of cancer.

> *Cigarette smoking is the single most destructive thing you can do to your health.*

The thing to keep in mind is that when you pick up a cigarette you are actively saying that smoking is more important than living, for you will not be able to do both for very long. If you smoke, *stop now!* If you don't smoke, *don't start!* 'Nuff said.

Now back to those other factors that put one at risk for heart attacks and coronary artery disease. What these factors all have in common is that they relate to being overweight.

Hypertension

One condition that causes heart attacks and coronary artery disease is hypertension—that is, high blood pressure. In a person with hypertension, the high pressure in the arteries of the heart destroy the inside lining of the artery, and this makes it easier for fatty cholesterol deposits to form and stick, which leads to a heart attack. As you know, one of the common causes of high blood pressure is being overweight or obese. So losing weight and treating the obesity lowers blood pressure, and at the same time lowers the risk of heart attack.

Cholesterol and Triglyceride Levels

Increased cholesterol and triglyceride levels greatly increase the risk of a heart attack, and they are also closely tied to excess body weight. Both cholesterol and triglyceride are forms of fat ("lipids" in medical terms). And both are necessary in order for the body to perform its numerous functions.

Cholesterol and triglycerides come from two different places: some are made by your own body and the rest come from the foods you eat. High levels of cholesterol are found in animal products and in foods with a lot of saturated fat, such as cheeses, meats, and whole milk. But simply having high cholesterol is only part of the picture. When doctors take your blood and run a cholesterol test, they aren't just looking at the total cholesterol level.

Right now, the cholesterol test reports four numbers.

The first number, total cholesterol levels, is self-explanatory. This figure includes all the different forms of cholesterol in the body. It's an important number, but by itself, the information it gives is limited.

Next is the LDL (or low density lipoprotein) level. This is also called "bad cholesterol." Having a high level of LDL cholesterol is a serious problem and is known eventually to lead to blockage of the arteries.

Then there is the HDL (or high density lipoprotein) level.

HDL is also known as the "good cholesterol." You want your HDL number to be as high as possible. Having a low HDL is just as much a risk factor for having coronary artery disease and heart attacks as having a high LDL. This is especially true in women. Unfortunately, not enough attention is paid to HDL, and often a low HDL is not treated aggressively.

Finally, there is the triglyceride level. Triglycerides have typically been ignored as an important aspect of heart disease risk, but high levels should be treated just like the other types of cholesterol are.

So what is a "healthy" cholesterol level? Well, that depends. (My sister is probably wondering why I can never give a straight answer.) It depends on how many other factors you have that put you at risk for blockage of the arteries. For example, if you have no family history of early heart disease (before age fifty), and you do not have high blood pressure, diabetes, or previous heart attack, and you do not smoke and are not obese, then your total cholesterol should be less than 200, your LDL less than 130, your HDL higher than 50, and your triglyceride level lower than 150.

On the other hand, if you have diabetes, you are at an increased risk of having blockage of the arteries and eventual heart attacks. Therefore, your LDL level should be lower than 100, your HDL should optimally be over 65, and triglycerides less than 130.

My guess is that, since you are reading this book, you likely have at least one and maybe several of the above risks for heart disease, so your optimal numbers are even lower. You should discuss with your doctor the optimal levels for you. Keep in mind that, just as diabetes complicates matters, so does heart disease. If you have ever had a heart attack, or have ever been diagnosed with coronary artery disease, then you must be treated with cholesterol-lowering drugs even if your numbers are in the optimal range.

Sedentary Lifestyles

Another reason you may be at risk for having blockage of the heart arteries is sedentary lifestyle. This is fancy language for "sitting on your butt too much." People who do not exercise and whose physical activity is limited (maybe because they spend hours at a time staring at the television or computer screen) are much more likely to develop the blockage of the arteries that eventually leads to heart attacks. Exercise, as we discussed earlier, lowers blood pressure. Exercise also has been shown to decrease cholesterol and triglyceride levels, thereby decreasing risk of heart attacks. Exercise also helps people to lose weight, which brings us back full circle: obesity is a central cause of coronary artery disease and heart attacks.

By now, you have likely gotten the picture on how being overweight or obese contributes indirectly to blockage of the arteries and heart attacks. You also understand how high blood pressure, high cholesterol, and sedentary lifestyles put people at risk. All these factors go back to being overweight.

Obesity

While obesity is the underlying cause of other risk factors, it is also a risk all by itself. Why? Obesity puts a mechanical burden on the heart (just recall the Ford Escort engine in the Cadillac truck). Obesity also contributes to insulin resistance. The insulin resistance in turn causes changes in the heart and the arteries that make blockage of the arteries and a heart attack much more likely. So directly (by forcing the heart to overwork to pump blood) or indirectly (by contributing to bad cholesterol levels, high blood pressure, and lack of exercise), obesity is a key component in the development of coronary artery disease and eventual heart attacks.

Are You an Apple or a Pear?

I am about to give you to some news that most of us will find exciting. What if I told you that where you put your fat matters when it comes to heart disease? Well, it seems to be true. Women who carry most of their weight in the stomach and waist area, referred to as "apple-shaped," are at a much greater risk for heart disease than those "pear-shaped" women whose obesity is focused in the legs, butt, and hip area. Good news for sisters, who often have an abundance of "junk in the trunk." But there's also a note of warning: Obese women before menopause are less likely than men to be apple-shaped. But after menopause, women tend to gain weight in a pattern similar to men. So it is not a coincidence that heart disease in women greatly increases after menopause.

It's easy to find out if you are an apple or a pear. If it is not obvious when you look in the mirror (are you fat up top with relatively skinny legs?), then you can figure out your waist-hip ratio. To do this, simply take a tape measure and measure your waist in inches. If you have trouble finding where your waist should be, stop. You are an apple. If you can find your waist, write that number down and measure the inches around your hips (take the widest area around your butt). Now divide the waist inches by the hip inches. If the number you get is more than 0.8, you are an apple and are at increased risk for heart disease and even diabetes. The waist-hip ratio is really just a number to discover whether your waist and hips are about the same width. (If you want to find out your waist-hip ration but don't want to do the math, go to:

http://tools.apollolife.com/waisthipratio/waisthipratio.asp

The bottom line is that all fat is not created equal. Fat that is stored mainly in the stomach area is much more dangerous than fat that is stored mainly in the hips and thighs.

There's a reason why this is so. An apple-shaped body type (or abdominal obesity) is dangerous because it contributes to a newly recognized condition called "the Metabolic Syndrome" or "Syndrome X." (Pay close attention, because this may describe you.) The Metabolic Syndrome describes a set of physical characteristics that are often seen together, and when seen together, often mean a greatly increased risk for heart disease and diabetes. The five features are:

1. Abdominal obesity (either a waist-to-hip ratio greater than 0.8 or a waist measurement of greater than 35 inches)

2. Elevated blood triglyceride level (greater than 150)

3. Low levels of HDL cholesterol (less than 50)

4. High blood pressure

5. A fasting blood sugar greater than 109

Why people with the above characteristics have such high rates of heart disease has not been completely figured out yet, but it is thought to be related to the way abdominal fat, much more than fat in the hips and thighs, makes substances that causes the body to respond poorly to insulin, as well as substances that cause blood pressure to rise and poor cholesterol levels to develop. So what does that mean for you if you are one of the Syndrome X types? It means that you need to be treated much more aggressively, with exercise, diet, and medications, even before heart complications develop.

Is That a Pain in My Chest?

Now, granted, my friend Lori was like me—on the thick side. But she was tall, and you would never look at her and think fat. She also had moderately high blood pressure. But really, whoever thinks that at forty she would have a heart attack? She felt fine. She looked fine. So how should she have known that she was at risk?

To know if you have coronary artery disease you must see a doctor. There are several tests that can be done if you are having symptoms, or if you are having no symptoms but are at an extremely high risk.

> To know if you have coronary artery disease you must see a doctor.

1) Your doctor might order a "stress test," which allows him or her to study your heart when it is beating fast and requiring a lot of blood and oxygen. In this way the doctor can learn if certain parts of the heart lack adequate blood flow. Stress tests are "indirect" tests, meaning they give us an indication that a certain artery is blocked, but we can't actually see the artery.

2) The "gold standard" (meaning the absolute best proof of heart disease) is the angiogram. The angiogram is a test in which a catheter is placed into a large artery (usually the artery in the

groin) and threaded up to the heart. Then dye is squirted into the heart vessels and, in real-time, the arteries of the heart are visualized. Each artery can be seen, and if they are blocked or partially blocked, they can be opened back up at the time of the angiogram. In this way the disease gets treated immediately at the time of diagnosis. There are risks to the procedure (such as kidney failure from the dye that is used), but it is often a very necessary test. For those with normal kidneys, the risks are low. However, if you have diabetes and/or diminished kidney function, the risks of kidney problems can be substantial, sometimes as much as 25 percent if the kidneys were not working well beforehand. The amount of dye used is also important—the less dye, the less risk. However, giving IV (intravenous) fluids and other treatments prior to the angiogram can greatly reduce the risk if the procedure is absolutely necessary.

When a person is actually having a heart attack (meaning heart muscle is dying), an EKG will also show certain changes and allow doctors to see the damage and provide immediate treatment.

Which brings us to the treatment and prevention of heart attacks. (The treatment *always* includes weight loss.)

Eight months after that phone call from Lori, a group of us met for vacation in Jamaica. Lori was healthy and feeling good, and her weight was down 35 pounds. After the heart attack, her doctor put her on a diet and exercise program—which she followed religiously. She looked good, and she felt great!

She was still on medication, and the doctor also prescribed "nitroglycerine" tablets for her to take when she had occasional chest pains. But the danger was over, and Lori seemed to come through the experience with better health and a new outlook on life.

Treatment and Prevention of Heart Attacks

In addition to weight loss, treatment for heart attacks typically includes medical management, meaning drug therapy. Also necessary in some cases is the surgical treatment angioplasty, in which the blocked vessel is forced open by the heart catheter. Cardiac stenting may also be necessary. A stent is a device placed inside the blocked vessel during the angiogram, and it stays there forever to help keep the vessel open.

Several studies have shown these procedures are not used enough in the black community and that minority patients often do poorly because of limited access to these procedures. The goal of these procedures is to restore blood flow to the heart so that more heart muscle can be saved. The most invasive treatment for blocked vessels is bypass surgery, where vessels from the leg or chest are used to "bypass" the blockage in the artery.

People who have had a heart attack need medical treatment and must begin exercise and weight loss programs. They must also stop using tobacco and be careful to control their blood pressure. Another part of their treatment will be medication. A small percentage of people can't take these drugs because of other health problems. But if you have had a heart attack and blocked arteries in the past and are not on these drugs, immediately ask your doctor why.

The first of these medications is a simple, everyday drug, but it saves lives. That drug is aspirin, an acetylsalicylic acid. One of the things aspirin does is to help keep blood flowing in the heart arteries and prevent blockage from occurring.

The second class of drug is called beta-blockers. They have been proven to help prevent future heart attacks in people who have had one in the past, and may also prevent a first heart attack in those with coronary disease.

The third class of drugs is called ACE inhibitors. They do many great things, like lowering blood pressure and helping to protect the kidneys in people with diabetes, but they also help restore heart function in people who have suffered a heart attack.

The fourth and last class of medicine you are likely to use if you've had a heart attack are called statins, and they are the closest thing we have to a miracle drug when it comes to heart disease. Statins are best known as cholesterol-lowering drugs. You have probably heard of them before, drugs such as Lipitor®, Zocor®, and Pravachol®. Anyone who has had a heart attack, or who has coronary artery disease, should be on this type of drug no matter what her cholesterol level is. That's right, even if you have a perfect cholesterol level, if you have had a heart attack in the past and blocked arteries, you should seriously consider—and ask your doctor—about taking this drug. There are some people, such as those with liver disease, who cannot take this type of medicine, but they are in the minority.

Statins don't just lower cholesterol; they also stabilize the cholesterol plaques that are already there. When the plaques are stable, they are much less likely to break off and completely block the artery, leading to a full-blown heart attack. Statins not only prevent heart attacks in people who have had them before, but they are also thought to prevent the first heart attack, as well as preventing strokes. So write these drugs down and ask your doctor about them.

If your doctor has not prescribed these drugs and you already have blockage of the arteries or have experienced a heart attack, make an appointment to discuss the drugs with your doctor. If, for whatever reason, the doctor still doesn't prescribe them, find another doctor.

You know, my friend Lori is just like us. Staying on a program of eating well and exercising is hard—it's a constant challenge. And for Lori, the challenges of school and work and taking care of a husband and children took their toll. She gained back almost all of the 35 pounds she'd lost.

She no longer felt as great. Her chest pains increased. And doctors were considering increasing her medications.

But Lori really understands that not staying on her program could mean the difference between life and death for her. So her program is, again, her first priority—before her husband, her kids, her schooling, or her work. Because if Lori doesn't put her health, diet, and exercise first, she'll be gone and everything else will be beside the point.

Lori's new goal? To be permanently "hoochie fine"!

I have no doubt that she'll be there again.

And just for support, we should ALL commit to being there with her!

Heart Disease Prevention and Treatment in a Nutshell

1. Know your blood pressure and discuss your blood pressure goals with your doctor.

2. Ask for a fasting cholesterol test, and know what your goal numbers are. If your cholesterol is high, treatment is needed.

3. If you have ever had a heart attack, or have been diagnosed with blocked arteries, you must consult your doctor about being put on a statin (cholesterol-lowering drug), aspirin, beta-blocker, and possibly an ACE inhibitor.

4. Know your target heart rate and discuss your exercise goals with your doctor before starting an exercise program.

Chapter Six   The Big "C" (Cancer)

In recent years, researchers have found a direct relation between cancer and obesity. Cancer. The "big C." If you're a black woman in this world, cancer has touched your life in some way—from the older relative who said before she saw any doctor at all, "just don't let 'em cut me," to our mothers and sisters and cousins and aunts battling breast cancer.

Most of us, when we hear the words, "I have lung cancer," let out a long sigh. "Us" doesn't just mean us African American women, either. We all know too many men who, once they reach middle age, develop prostate cancer.

In fact, Stacy and I had our first experiences with cancer when our grandfather was diagnosed with cancer of the prostate. It was devastating for us all. But I'll let Stacy speak for herself.

My grandfather (whom we affectionately called Papa) was the cement that held our family together. His children and grandchildren were his life, and he loved us all dearly. But honestly (and don't tell Teri), everyone knew I was his favorite. My Papa was an active man, who picked me up from school each day and went out every weekend in his boat to go fishing. Then, suddenly, it was my father picking me up from school and the boat was permanently docked. Around that time, we were finally told that Papa had cancer, and he was going to California to get treatment.

In my young mind, everything seemed to happen like a movie stuck in the fast forward mode. The cancer demons swooped down and carried my grandfather off to virtually another planet to die (we Texans have always considered California part of another universe).

For a long time after that, my image of cancer was associated with inevitability and loss of control. Cancer, as I saw it, turned people into victims. Those struck down by mysterious tumors were kind of like farmers randomly struck down by lightning: you were simply powerless against it.

There are things that we do and choices we make that increase our chances of developing this terrible disease.

Many years and a medical degree later, I realize that the perceptions held by me and many of our community are not necessarily true. Granted, there is still some "randomness" associated with various forms of cancer, because science and medicine don't have all the answers as to why some cancers happen. But there are things that we do and choices we make that increase our chances of developing this terrible disease.

We are not necessarily helpless in the face of the big C. In fact, more and more people are finding ways to survive cancer, through their own efforts along with the efforts of their doctors

More and more people are finding ways to survive cancer, through their own efforts along with the efforts of their doctors and technicians.

and technicians. But a lot of people still won't see it, or even look at it. Sometimes it's easier and more comforting to believe that there is nothing we can do or could have done to help ourselves. It is a hard thing to own up to our part in developing one of these illnesses, or to our part in learning to manage and possibly even cure it. Being a victim is oftentimes more comfortable, and let's be honest, it requires no work or effort on our part. Why work if there's no hope? But the fact is, there's plenty of hope, if we just look at the facts and use our common sense.

And now—surprise, surprise—the cancer that's been in our community for years is being linked to obesity.

You know, I read articles and see television segments about the links between weight and cancer all the time. But exactly how that link is made is never fully explained. I mean, they say it, and we hear it. But we aren't shown a connection that we can understand unless we have a medical degree. So we're going to do something different in this chapter. I'm going to ask the Doc to take us through this step-by-step, and connect all the dots. Because hearing it is one thing, understanding enough to make informed decisions is quite another.

I'm setting only one rule for Stacy: We ask, she answers . . . no "medicalese" allowed! Sound good?

All right, let's hear it!

Some Facts About Cancer, the Community, and Late Diagnosis

I know you think you have heard it all. This damn doctor has been trying to blame everything but the kitchen sink on weight, and now she's even blaming cancers on being fat!

People seem more ready to see the connections between obesity and diabetes or heart disease. But they find the connection between obesity and cancer is just too much. To be completely honest with you, when scientific news first surfaced associating fat to cancer, I, too, was a little skeptical. But years— and several studies later—we've made remarkable leaps in our understanding of the disease process. Once you understand the process of cancer—what it is and how it works—I think you'll see that the link with obesity is nothing but the truth.

Come on, are you telling us that all cancers are related to obesity?

No, that's not what I'm saying. Not all cancers are related to obesity, but many of the major killers are. Cancers of the colon, breast, prostate, ovary, uterus and kidneys appear to be associated with obesity. The National Cancer Institute estimates that obesity is responsible for approximately 130,000 cases of cancer in this country every year.

Cancer statistics, especially in the black community, are alarming. There are approximately 130,000 new diagnoses of

---

The National Cancer Institute estimates that obesity is responsible for approximately 130,000 cases of cancer in this country every year.

---

cancer made each year among African Americans, and 64,000 of us die of various types of cancer each year.

Cancers, especially of the prostate, breast, and colon, tend to be at more advanced stages in African Americans before they are treated. That is, they are diagnosed later. In many of these cases, had the patient sought medical help earlier, the illness could have been treated far more effectively. Regular medical checkups could have ensured that early diagnosis and treatment. Advanced-stage cancers tend to be more aggressive and more deadly.

The reasons why many of us don't get to the doctor for regular checkups are still being widely debated. Many say that African Americans don't have as ready access to health care, and that's why we get to the doctor later than people of other ethnic groups.

While ready access to health care explains part of the problem, it doesn't explain it all. For example, we now know, after many years of research, that there are differences between certain ethnic groups in the way cancers behave and how these cancers respond to treatment.

But it's also true that African Americans, as a group, tend to be fatter, lead more unhealthy lifestyles, and have diets more likely to consist of a lot of fatty foods. Obesity and unhealthy diet not only play a role in developing our cancers, but they also contribute to a lot of other health problems (like heart disease and diabetes) that make getting effective treatment and surviving cancer less likely.

There it is: less ready access to health care and genetics stand on one side of the problem. You certainly can't change your genetics, and, unless you're a miracle worker, you're not likely to improve the national medical system immediately, however much it might need improving.

What you can do is to recognize the facts:

- African Americans have a 33 percent higher death rate from cancer than white Americans.
- Two of the top three most common cancers in black women (breast cancer makes up 31 percent of all cancer diagnoses and colon cancer makes up 12 percent) are strongly associated with obesity and diets high in fat.

Several other cancers, such as cancer of the uterus and ovaries, although not quite as common, are also believed to be highly influenced by body fat. So no, not all cancers are related to obesity, but as you can see, the most common ones, breast and colon, are.

I think that before we move on you need to give us a better idea of what cancer is and how it works. You gave me a definition of cancer recently, and I thought it was hilarious.

Yeah, cancer is like your Aunt Betty's bad-ass kids. They don't listen and no one can control them. Here's how that works in your body. The body is made up of cells—the "building blocks of the body." And when cells are grouped together, they form our internal organs—our heart and liver and kidneys and skin. Cancer is the uncontrolled growth of abnormal cells. Cancer happens when certain cells of the body no longer pay attention to instructions to stop growing. Normal cells only multiply and grow to a certain

Cancer is the uncontrolled growth of abnormal cells.

point, and then their "internal time clock" signals that it is time for the cell to stop growing. The cell then dies and is replaced with a new one.

What makes a cell "behave badly" in the first place is a mutation, or alteration, of a normal cell. That's what makes mutated cells grow uncontrollably. It's the mutation that makes the cell behave very badly and not listen anymore.

Now, mutations happen all the time. There are trillions of cells in the body, all growing and dividing constantly, so the odds favor an occasional random mutation. But the human body is quite remarkable, and when one of these "abnormal" cells occurs, the immune system ordinarily finds it quickly and gobbles it up (picture Pacman and you've got the idea).

The immune system is a highly efficient defense system, but it's not perfect Should a bad cell happen to slip by the immune system, then it will quickly multiply, make more bad cells, and eventually these cells combine to cause a cancer.

"Well, if mutation itself doesn't start a cancer, what else is needed?

Scientists believe in the "two-hit theory" of cancer development. This means that at least two separate events or circumstances must occur in order for a cancer to develop. The mutation that slips past the immune system is one hit. The "second hit," as we will explain soon, is often something within your control.

I'm not quite ready to leave mutations. You never said anything about how they begin.

Carcinogens

There's still a lot we don't know, but I'll tell you what we *do* know. Some mutations, like the mutation that is found in about

5 percent of breast cancers are inherited from your parents in the form of a "gene." (So yeah, she does get it from her mamma.) In fact, the "breast cancer gene" was discovered in families with high rates of breast cancer, and people from such families got cancer at fairly young ages.

Another major reason for mutations is exposure to cancer-causing substances, called "carcinogens." We currently know of thousands of chemicals that cause cancer, including those found in cigarette smoke. Carcinogens are also present in the fumes from automobiles and gasoline, and even in the chemicals used to dry clean your clothes or bleach your kitchen sink. So yes, they are everywhere.

Well, about carcinogens, it seems that every time you read or turn on the TV still another thing is linked to cancer—the air, pesticides, hormones in meat, fertilizer, the water. Is everything a carcinogen?

It's true, we are surrounded by carcinogens, and scientists are finding new ones all the time. Even certain viruses, like the hepatitis C virus, are known to be carcinogens. There are many other carcinogens we breathe in each day and consume in our food. But that exposure is just a possible first step down the road to cancer. It is simply the trigger that causes the initial cell mutation to happen.

Remember that a cancer is the uncontrollable growth of an abnormal cell, so carcinogens get the ball rolling, but other things are needed to keep that bad mutated cell dividing and growing. This is the fascinating part of cancer research—trying to figure out how to control the "second hit" in the two-hit theory of cancer development. We can't do much about genetics—not at this time. We can help control carcinogens by eating right, but in general, they too are beyond your control as an individual.

But eating right and avoiding obesity is a way to create an environment unfavorable to cancer cells. By eating a proper diet and controlling weight, we have the most power to control our own medical destinies.

> *By eating a proper diet and controlling weight, we have the most power to control our own medical destinies.*

It's funny . . . Stacy and I have never talked much about cancer. We're young, relatively healthy, and we understand that most cancers don't hit young women—black or white—very often. So, there's a tendency to assume that it simply doesn't apply to us.

We both know better than that these days. But I still have a lot to learn. I mean, there's a push these days to blame EVERY illness currently known to man on being overweight and on obesity—including cancer. I'm beginning to feel like overeating has become the new "smoking." But I still don't get the link. How does fat change our bodies and lead to cancer?

Okay, okay, I hear you. My sister means well, but she has always been impatient. She's the type to read the first chapter of a book and then skip to the end. But I aim to please, so let's get back to business.

Cancer and Body Fat

Fat is thought to be a factor in developing cancer in three main ways.

1. The Fat Factory

The first way fat contributes to cancer development has to do with the fat itself. Fat just doesn't "sit there" and do nothing. It is actually very busy (even if the person it's living on isn't). Fat is like a "hormone factory" in that it makes large amounts of hormones, such as estrogen and insulin. Insulin is a growth hormone that causes cells to reproduce more rapidly, and when normal cells multiply more than they should, the chances are greater that a mutation will occur.

The immune system can usually destroy these bad cells, but if there are too many, the body's defenses can be overwhelmed. So the more fat you have, the more hormones you produce and the greater the chance that a cancerous cell (one with a mutation) will develop. To make matters worse, not only do the hormones made by fat increase the chances of a cancer cell occurring, but once it does occur, the hormones also help make the cancer grow and spread.

This is especially true for female cancers like breast, uterine, and ovarian cancers, which have been directly linked to the effects of too much estrogen. Take breast cancer for instance. When people began to study breast cancer seriously, in the 1970s, they noticed that this cancer was more common in women who started their periods at very young ages (for example, ten years old) and went into menopause at very old ages (mid-fifties). Women who had never given birth also had higher breast cancer rates than those women who had had several children.

What all these women turned out to have in common was that they had more menstrual periods over their lifetimes. Someone who starts her period at age ten had almost fifty more periods than someone who starts at age fourteen. And a woman who enters menopause at fifty-five has over a hundred more cycles than a woman who starts menopause at forty-six.

And it's just the opposite for women who have several children. Obviously, you don't have menstrual cycles while pregnant, so for each child, that is nine or ten fewer periods over your lifetime.

Okay, that was the windup. Here's the pitch. With every menstrual period, a woman is exposed to a big surge of the hormone estrogen that happens around the middle of the cycle. A large amount of estrogen is needed to make the ovary release an egg (called "ovulation"). To make a long story short, what these women who had early periods, late menopause, and no kids had in common was more exposure to estrogen over their lifetimes.

As scientists tried to figure out the cancer-estrogen relationship, they discovered that many cancers, including breast, ovarian, and uterine cancers, produce substances that enable them to grow uncontrollably, and estrogen is involved in making all of this happen. How this happens is quite complex, but just understand that there is a strong estrogen-cancer relationship.

Now we're sliding into home base. Fat cells make estrogen. And the more fat cells you have, the more estrogen you make. This is one of the main reasons that being obese greatly increases your chances of developing cancer.

2. Stuck on You

The second way that fat causes cancer is by holding on to chemicals and carcinogens. Yes, we eat and breathe in thousands of cancer-causing substances every day. However, in a healthy body these are usually quickly eliminated or destroyed by the immune system. But fat cells like to hold on to carcinogens longer than they should. This gives the carcinogens more time to hang out in the body and cause havoc.

So the more fat you have, the more exposure you have to cancer-causing agents, and the chances of mutations also increase. Potentially, this could be a problem in numerous cancers. There are ways to get the carcinogens out of your system (more about that later), but fat makes the fight more challenging.

3. Fat Food vs. Healthy Food

The last two ways fat and obesity contribute to cancer are strictly lifestyle issues. The first and probably most important is poor diet. Poor diet is directly linked to cancer. Period. You can't get around it. What do we mean by "poor" diets? These are diets typical of Western countries such as the United States that are high in processed foods (chips, lunch meats, white bread, etc.), and that are also high in red meats and fried foods.

A long time ago, scientists noticed that certain cancers, especially cancer of the colon, were practically unheard of in non-Westernized Asian and African countries. I say "non-Westernized" because guess what happened when Asian and African people came to the United States and started eating the typical American diet? That's right. They started to develop colon cancer just like we did. Skeptics then said that maybe it was something in the air, or whatever, that was causing the cancer, not necessarily the diet.

But there's still more evidence that diet is the core culprit. Now that America-style fast food restaurants and other kinds of fast food have entered Asian and African cities, guess what? It turns out that when people eat these foods, colon cancer rates increase.

Fried foods and fatty foods can and do play a role in some of the most fatal cancers—especially cancers of the colon and breast. We don't yet know how this works, but we do know it works: There is a 50 percent increase in colon cancer risk among women who eat a lot of fried, processed, and fatty foods.

While we don't yet know precisely why, we have some strong theories. We believe that the frying (especially deep-frying) process produces harmful carcinogens. If you eat too much of these foods, you are likely to be overweight or obese, and as we said previously, your fat cells themselves will make hormones that contribute to the development of cancers.

But that's just the bad news. The good news is that, just as there are harmful, cancer-causing food habits, there are also diets that fight the development of cancers. These diets are high in fruits, vegetables, and whole grains—all substances that ward off cancers (as well as diabetes and heart disease). Again, we haven't figured out all the whys and hows, but we have some compelling theories. A big one is the theory about antioxidants.

Antioxidants are substances found in foods such as green vegetables and whole fruits. Here is how they work to fight cancer: Exposure to everyday pollution, smoke, and other common chemicals produces "free radicals." No, free radicals are not revolutionaries released from jail. They are molecules that destroy the body's DNA. When this happens, it opens the door to mutations, and these bad, mutated cells are the beginnings of cancer. Antioxidants shut down production of these free radicals, and therefore decrease mutations.

Where do you find these antioxidants? If you say "on the shelf at the drugstore," you need some serious dietary counseling. Vitamins such as vitamin C, A, E, and beta-carotene are antioxidants, and they are available as "dietary supplements." But the best place to get these vitamins is in fresh fruits and vegetables like broccoli, spinach, blueberries, apples, and green beans, to name a few. The benefits of eating these foods are far greater than what you get from taking a vitamin a day. We aren't sure why; perhaps there are substances in food that cannot completely be reproduced in a pill.

The best place to get these vitamins is in fresh fruits and vegetables like broccoli, spinach, blueberries, apples, and green beans, to name a few.

As to how we can get rid of fat: exercise is a natural fat flusher. Not only does exercise prevent the buildup of fat, but since fat also increases insulin levels in the body (remember, insulin promotes the occurrence and growth of cancer cells), exercise helps our bodies get rid of all the carcinogens we eat and breath. It does so by boosting metabolism and speeding up all those body processes that clear out the bad stuff. Of course, the less exposure to cancer-causing agents, the better.)

But Let's Be Real. Not Only Fat People Get Cancer

Some things in life you simply can't control—they "just happen." Certain cancers fall into this category. But many cancers happen because of what we do. I won't even begin to mention cigarette smoking, because we have already established that it is just plain suicidal. But being overweight and adopting unhealthy lifestyles (like eating fast foods or getting no exercise) can be just as dangerous.

Then what's your move? Again you guessed it. By losing weight and getting regular exercise, you can prevent many cancers and feel better in the process.

Of course, it is very important to get screened for cancer whether you are fat or skinny. This means getting yearly mammograms, having a colonoscopy every five years starting at age fifty (sooner if you have a family history of colon cancer), and also making sure to have yearly Pap smears and pelvic exams.

True, being fit and healthy won't guarantee that you won't get cancer. But if you do ever have the disease, being at a good weight and keeping fit make you better able to fight it. You're a better "contender" if your body is strong.

Stacy told you earlier about our Pap, and she mentioned our other grandfather and his prostate cancer as well. Let me tell you about him. We called him Granddaddy. Since I was his and my grandmother's first grandchild, and since I spent most of my time as a little girl with them, I was of course—his favorite. (I have to say that, but, honestly, I think our cutest, quietest cousin, Lynne, had us both trumped!)

Granddaddy was blind. He lost his sight to glaucoma early on, but you'd never know it. He went to work every day, he cooked dinner, he took his coffee black with sugar, he sang in the church choir, and his hearing was so sharp you'd almost think it was sight!! I always looked forward to the time of day when Granny and I picked him up from work at the Lighthouse.

His family was his world, and he would sit in "his" chair by the door of the house smoking a pipe. I was very young when he died. But what I remember most was that Granddaddy was proud and he was stubborn and he did things his way always. In fact, so proud was he that he never, ever told my grandmother about his cancer. She didn't find out until it had spread into his bones, all over his body. And then, he refused to have surgery.

Today, Granddaddy would have different options and make better choices.

So you see, like most black families, the Mitchell sisters' lives have been touched by cancer. We know from experience that all cancers aren't caused by obesity. In fact, the cancer that has touched our lives had nothing to do with obesity or women. But cancer is cancer, and the effects on any family, no matter the cause, is devastating.

So if there is anything that can be done to save a family or anyone at all from the sadness of this disease, it should be done. And if there are measures we can take to help stave off cancer, we should take them. Stacy and I owe it to our Granddaddy and Papa, and you owe it to your loved ones.

Chapter Seven

It Takes My Breath Away (Respiratory Illness)

When I was seven or eight, my sister, who was quite demanding (and a little spoiled if you ask me), had a way of "asking" me for things. She would sit on my chest until I couldn't breathe. After what seemed like an eternity of gasping and laughing and choking and screaming, I often just gave up and agreed to give her what she wanted, which was usually money.

What does all this have to do with obesity? Well, as you continue to read about the effects that fat can have on your respiratory (breathing) system, imagine the sensation of someone sitting on your chest, and it will make understanding much simpler. (Of course, if you already have a respiratory illness, you won't have to imagine.)

The respiratory system controls our breathing. It is responsible for "gas exchange" into and out of our bodies—which means bringing air into the lungs (inhaling), transferring all the oxygen out of the air and into the blood, then releasing the "deoxygenated" air back into the environment (exhaling). All of this goes on each time you draw a breath and then release it.

The lungs are where most of the serious business of the breathing process occurs. But the respiratory system involves *all* the parts of the body exposed to air as it makes its way into the lungs. So the nose, mouth, and throat (called the "upper" airway) are important as well. Further, the heart and lungs are physically connected and work together to ensure that fresh oxygen gets to all parts of the body. So diseases of the lungs can lead to problems with the heart as well.

Restrictive Lung Disease

When you see a big person huffing and puffing, it is no coincidence that he or she is usually out of breath and tired. Sometimes, this is simply because that person is out of shape. But often the breathlessness and fatigue are due to changes that occur in the lungs as a result of carrying around all the excess weight.

Restrictive lung disease is one of the consequences of obesity. And it is exactly as it sounds.

For just a minute, I want you to stop. Pay attention to your breathing. Do you notice how, when you inhale, your chest lifts up and out? This is because your lungs are expanding as the outside air is rushing in, just as they will contract when they push the air out. It is critically important that your lungs expand fully and oxygen gets to the entire lung, including the very bottom parts. The entire lung must be filled in order for there to be enough oxygen to distribute throughout your body.

Restrictive lung disease happens when the lungs are no longer being used fully because something is keeping them from filling and is obstructing the chest from moving outward. In cases of obesity, what keeps the lungs from inflating is fat. In other words, there is someone sitting on your chest twenty-four hours a day! And just as I had problems breathing after five minutes of big sis on my chest, you can have those same difficulties if you carry around too much upper body fat.

Here's how it works. It takes enormous energy even for the lungs of a normal-weight person to fill when she breathes in. For someone who is overweight, the lungs have to work still harder. When it becomes *too* hard for the lungs to expand fully and bring in all the oxygen the body needs, the lungs "sacrifice"—that is, the very bottoms of the lungs simply shut down.

It is the same as if you lived in a ten-bedroom mansion in upstate New York (just pretend, okay?). It's the middle of winter, and five below zero outside. You live in the house alone, but only use two of the ten rooms, and heating the entire mansion is getting darn expensive. So what do you do? You close off the parts of the house you don't use and concentrate all the heat and electricity on the two rooms you do use. Makes sense, doesn't it?

When parts of the lungs get "closed off," you obviously have less lung function, meaning there is less space for oxygen exchange. As a result, you get short of breath. At first, you experience the shortness of breath only when you are exerting yourself. Eventually, you will feel it even when you are sitting and doing nothing.

The shortness of breath is bad enough. But still another harmful thing happens when parts of the lungs are not exposed to oxygen. The lungs collapse in those areas and, over time, scarring occurs. This scarring creates a perfect setup for pneumonias and other infections. And the dangerous process all started because of the overabundance of fat you carry around the chest.

Treatment for long-standing restrictive lung disease is not very promising. There is a method called "positive pressure ventilation," in which you wear an "oxygen mask" that delivers oxygen at greater pressures. What this does is to force air down into your lungs with enough pressure to overcome the weight of all that chest and abdominal fat. This treatment is as uncomfortable as it sounds. That is why losing weight is the better, healthier treatment.

For lung patients who don't lose weight and who continue to lose lung function, the treatment required may eventually be "mechanical ventilation," a procedure in which a tube is put in your throat and a machine delivers the oxygen directly to your lungs. Not all obese people end up like this, but it's one possible outcome, and it is entirely preventable.

Obstructive Sleep Apnea

Restrictive lung disease is not the only consequence of obesity, and it's not the most common one, either. A much more common breathing problem that causes serious problems but is under-diagnosed is obstructive sleep apnea, and its most common symptom is the sometimes ordinary act of snoring.

I snore. Now, I've never been diagnosed with sleep apnea, but if you ask Stacy, she'll tell you that she just doesn't want to be around me when I'm sleeping. She claims I snore. Really, it's not just a claim. I know I do. How do I know? There have been times when I've woken myself up with snoring. Lovely, right?

Anyway, lately I've been looking for the "cure." Some wonderful, new, over-the-counter solutions have recently appeared on the market:

potions and sprays and face contraptions that stop snoring instantly.
My next new purchase is going to be something that can cure this
problem for good. But when I ask my sister about these "treatments,"
all she says is "lose weight." Well, that's obviously on my "to do" list
But until then I need something to fix the snoring. Why? Because
snoring is bad for my love life!

Teri herself doesn't suffer from one of the more serious forms
snoring can take, so she can worry just about how snoring affects
her love life. But where snoring is a symptom of obstructive sleep
apnea, the condition becomes serious and potentially deadly.

Obstructive sleep apnea happens while you are asleep, but
some of the problems it causes carry over to the daylight hours as
well. *Apnea* means, "not breathing." And this is what occurs
during sleep. Someone with sleep apnea has frequent periods
during the night when he or she stops breathing. After several
seconds and sometimes even one or two minutes, the person
wakes up and starts breathing again, and the cycle of falling
asleep, stopping breathing, and waking up continues to repeat
itself throughout the night.

Not only is this cycle highly disruptive of sleep, but during
the "apneic" periods (when you stop breathing) your body's
oxygen falls to very low levels. This chronic low oxygen level
causes all kinds of bad things to happen. (There are even
psychiatric and emotional consequences of poor sleep and lack of
oxygen.)

The most serious consequence of low oxygen levels during
the night is that people with sleep apnea often get very low heart
rates during the "non-breathing" episodes. Sometimes the heart
beats so slowly and irregularly that a heart attack or even sudden
death can result. Some scientists believe that sleep apnea may

actually be the cause of many people dying in their sleep. But for those who don't die suddenly, the low levels of oxygen and the subsequent high levels of other gases (like carbon dioxide) in the body make the blood vessels in the heart and lungs constrict, or get smaller.

As you may recall, when arteries get smaller and stiffer, the result is hypertension (aka high blood pressure). And sleep apnea, when it is not treated and controlled, is a cause of hypertension, along with heart attacks, strokes, or kidney failure.

Most people with sleep apnea also have leg swelling. This is because the weakened heart is no longer effective in moving fluids throughout the body. Fluids then build up in the legs, in the lungs (making it even harder to breath), and sometimes in the abdomen.

Sleep apnea is serious and potentially deadly. But what people who have this disorder seem to notice even more than the physical problems are the psychological and emotional consequences. An important feature of sleep apnea is excessive sleepiness during the day, in part because of poor sleep at night. In addition, the low oxygen levels and high carbon dioxide levels at night carry over to the daytime as well, and this contributes to the constant feeling of fatigue.

Now I know that lots of people reading this are thinking that they must have sleep apnea because they are tired and sleepy all the time. But with sleep apnea, the fatigue is severe. People complain of falling asleep in the middle of work, or while eating, writing or—and this is the dangerous one—driving. You can see that we're talking about something more serious than just feeling tired. Chronic fatigue brought on by sleep apnea may also result in memory loss, depression, and other behavioral and emotional problems caused by the long-term lack of oxygen and poor sleep.

Let's be honest—black women lose sleep and wrestle with memory loss and depression in high numbers with or without sleep apnea. And many of us who don't have sleep apnea still snore because of excess weight.

Call me superficial. But it seems to me that the aesthetics of snoring is much more unappealing than the medical problems. Have you ever watched someone snore? I mean, really snore? One of those mouth-open, bulldozer-sounding, deep-wall-rattling snores? And have you ever seen— actually seen—one of those snores come from a lady? It just isn't pretty.

I've always been a fan of fairy tales. And I've always dreamed of being Sleeping Beauty, and the Prince comes to wake me up with a kiss. But before he kisses me, he watches me blissfully slumber, and I'm beautiful. (Yes, I watch a lot of movies).

But can you imagine a Princess sprawled out on her back and snoring like a lineman? That would kind of ruin the perfect moment, wouldn't it? Fairy tale or not, the same thing happens all too commonly in ordinary life.

Thanks, Sleeping Beauty. We can probably all agree that snoring isn't very pretty, but now I want to explain how fat helps create that ugly picture. Maybe I can get you to see that what's at stake here is even more important than your love life.

Remember that the full name of the snoring disorder is obstructive sleep apnea. The obstruction to lungs, nasal passages, and throat is due to fat. When you sleep, all the muscles in your body relax and lose most of their tone. The muscles of the upper airway are no exception. These are the muscles that, when you are awake, are responsible for keeping your airway open. So when you sleep and those muscles relax, there is the potential for these structures to "collapse" and block the airway, meaning no air is getting in, and you stop breathing.

If you understand this, then you can easily see why having a lot of fat located around the neck, chin, and face area, is a big risk. All that weight and fat collapses your airway when you sleep, and the series of bad events starts to happen. (Also keep in mind that you can have fat-related "obstruction" that causes snoring without it having advanced enough to meet the definition of actual sleep apnea.)

The definitive test for sleep apnea is a "sleep study," where you go to a center or hospital overnight, and while you sleep, your oxygen levels are monitored, along with your heart rhythm and breathing patterns. But before your doctor can decide if sleep apnea is a possibility, he or she will ask you questions about signs you may be experiencing.

While most people who snore do not have sleep apnea, most everyone with sleep apnea snores. Snoring can indicate that the upper airway is partially collapsing, and when the air is forced through these partially collapsed structures, there is a loud and (to anyone in the vicinity) annoying sound. Often, it is the husband, wife, or partner of the person with sleep apnea who notices that the sleeping person stops breathing frequently during the night, and often the spouse or partner has to wake the snorer up so that he or she will breath again.

Your doctor will also ask you about other symptoms, including:

- Extreme daytime sleepiness, such as falling asleep in the middle of tasks or even while talking
- Memory loss
- Depression
- Other emotional problems

Remember that these can also be symptoms of a lot of other conditions as well. That's why it's so important to see a doctor for the diagnosis. With treatment, some patients find that the psychological symptoms, even disabling depression, vanish along with the snoring.

If your doctor suspects sleep apnea, he or she will send you for a sleep study, during which your breathing, heart rate and rhythm, and oxygen levels are closely watched. Based on the results, your doctor can tell if sleep apnea is the problem. If so, it would be good news because apnea is treatable.

Your doctor will suggest that you use a "positive pressure" breathing machine called CPAP at night to force air into the lungs and keep the upper airway from collapsing. It doesn't make the sleeping experience very pleasant, and the mask you have to wear will likely put the brakes on any late-night romance you had planned.

Now we're back to fat being bad for your love life. I want to tell you a really funny story. A man I was involved with simply refused to sleep in the same room with me. He was a light sleeper, and initially, "when love was new," he tried to rough it out. In fact, he tried for quite a while, I've got to give that to him. But sleeping in the same room with me snoring made him so tired the next day that eventually he just couldn't do it. So when I visited, he slept in one room and I slept in another. We got along great, we had a great time—but any dreams I had about waking up in the arms of that particular Prince Charming were on hold until the snoring was under control.

The ultimate treatment in cases of snoring or apnea caused by excess fat is to lose weight. That treatment can prevent the conditions I've discussed—before the lungs and heart undergo irreversible changes.

Well, this medical talk is informative, but for me it doesn't speak to the bottom line: how sleep apnea and restricted lung capacity can seriously hurt the quality of your life. We all want to be able to run and play with our kids, or be able to make love to our partners without wheezing and gasping for air. And we don't want to miss out on those long walks holding hands because we can't walk around the block without huffing and puffing.

Close your eyes and imagine something with me.

You're on an island with your significant other. You take a long walk to a deserted part of the beach carrying a picnic basket. The water seems to surround you, the sky is perfectly blue and clear, and far into the distance you can see the place where the ocean seems to meet the sky. You run and frolic and play in the water (never getting tired) and then dash back up to the blanket to get warm. He builds you a bonfire and you have a picnic dinner—complete with wine—by the light of the crackling fire. It's a warm night. The moon is full and the sky sparkles with stars. After dark, you sit and watch the waves by moonlight, falling asleep in his arms. You are beautiful. So beautiful, in fact, that he is completely enamored and stays up all night with his arms wrapped around you, watching you sleep. And while you are sleeping, no sounds can be heard but the rolling of the waves and your quiet, peaceful breathing.

Chapter Eight   Aches and Pains: Joint Disease

Here is an actual conversation between a patient and me. (Names have been changed to protect the oblivious, the stubborn, and those in perpetual denial). And, no, this is not my sister.

Jane Doe: Hi, Dr. Mitchell.

Doc: Hello, how are you today?

Jane Doe: Horrible. It's my knees. They're still hurting all the time, and I can barely walk. The medicine you gave me last time isn't working anymore. It did okay at first, but the pain is getting worse.

Doc: Remember when we discussed your obesity and how your knees are rebelling against having to carry around all that weight? I can't help but notice that you have gained another fifteen pounds since the last time I saw you. So it doesn't surprise me that your knees are getting more painful.

Jane Doe: Yes, I know, I know. But I think you blame everything on my weight instead of giving me medicine that could give me some relief from what's seriously wrong with me. And now the pain has spread to my back. I have pain in my back when I'm sitting down, and I stand up to relieve the pain and my knees hurt and give out. I think I need to be in the hospital.

Doc (to herself): Yeah, a mental hospital.

Jane Doe: We need to find out what is wrong. I was looking up my symptoms on the Internet and here is a list of things that are possibly wrong with me. We should make sure that we've ruled out these things before we place the blame on my weight.

Doc (reading from the list Jane Doe has given her): ruptured abdominal aortic aneurysm, Lyme disease, metastatic prostate cancer? Sorry, but you don't even have a prostate. You're a woman.

Jane Doe: Really? Okay, what about the other things on the list?

Doc: Look, when I was in medical school, my instructors used to tell us that when you hear hooves, think horses, not zebras.

Jane Doe: So?

Doc: Meaning that you should explore the obvious causes first before you start thinking of the rare and obscure.

Jane Doe: Okay, Doc, here's the deal. If it happens to be something on the list I just gave you, we can get me some medicine and fix the problem. If not . . . let's assume that you're right, and I'm not necessarily saying that you are, but suppose that it is my weight. My joints hurt so bad that I can't do anything to try to lose the weight, so I get bigger because all I can do is sit all day, and the bigger I get, the more my joints hurt. So what am I supposed to do?

Jane, although deeply consumed by denial, has just described the major problem in treating this painful, debilitating complication of obesity known as *arthritis*. Arthritis is a broad term that refers to disease and inflammation of the joints. To most people, arthritis simply means pain. But it is much more than that.

Arthritis is a disease of the joints. A joint is where the ends of two or more bones meet. In between those bones is cartilage, a smooth substance, around 2 millimeters thick, which covers the ends of the joint in a healthy individual. Cartilage is something that no one really thinks about until it's gone. It acts as a cushion to prevent bones from grinding together. Consider it the "shock absorber" of your skeleton, and the changes that occur in the joint and lead to arthritis all begin with the cartilage. This is where the action is. When the cartilage wears down, the pain of arthritis is the inevitable result.

For as long as I've known her—which is my entire life—my Granny Ophelia has had bad feet and bad legs. Or at least that's what I thought when I was little. It's actually bad ankles and bad knees. (I know Stacy and I talk about our grandparents a lot! But as for most black children, our grandparents have always been part of our immediate family and a big part of our lives and life lessons.)

Granny has always been a healthy woman, but as she got older her ankles and her knees got worse and worse. They would really hurt her. Even as a child I knew that. I remember her coming home and, first thing, taking off her shoes and rubbing her ankles and legs down because they hurt so badly.

There are over a hundred different types of arthritis, and thousand-page texts fall short in explaining them all. So we're not going to try. (Teri is pleased.) Instead, we are going to stick to arthritis and its relation to being fat. But first I need to stress one point. Although only one type of arthritis is caused by obesity, all types are made worse by excess weight, and the more pounds, the worse the arthritis.

Now, many types of arthritis are autoimmune diseases. These autoimmune forms of arthritis include:

- Rheumatoid arthritis
- Arthritis caused by lupus
- Arthritis associated with severe forms of the skin condition psoriasis.

"Autoimmune" means that, for reasons we don't fully understand, the body begins to attack certain parts of itself. In the case of autoimmune arthritis, the body's immune system attacks the joints and they become worn down and destroyed.

Although these types of joint disease are not caused by obesity, excess weight quickens the eventual destruction of the joint, causing more pain and even more severe arthritis, especially for people with arthritis caused by an autoimmune disorder,

The type of arthritis that *is* caused by obesity is osteoarthritis (also called OA, for short). It is often referred to as "degenerative joint disease" (although this is not really the proper term for it) and is the most common joint disease that we know of. Osteoarthritis is also a leading cause of disability in this country.

All of the pain in Granny's legs started out "innocently enough."

According to Granny, she was sauntering down the street in high-heeled shoes one day—as all good "divas" do—when her heel got caught and she badly sprained her ankle. She was put in a cast, but she didn't wear it for the full time prescribed by the doctor, so the ankle never healed properly. In fact, if you look at her ankle it's permanently "rolled in." That injury, combined with wear-and-tear on her knees from playing basketball as a young woman, made Granny a prime candidate for arthritis. Add in the fact that she was overweight, and you have a complete recipe for pain that will get worse over the years.

Osteoarthritis can be caused by a previous injury that damaged the once healthy cartilage so that it doesn't function properly. It can also be caused by repetitive stress, as from jobs that require a specific, constant motion (think: factory assembly line). Athletes are also candidates for OA. For instance, professional baseball pitchers can get arthritis in the elbow joint (which is very uncommon in the rest of the population), and ballet dancers can get OA in the ankle joint. But since you are reading this book about obesity, chances are you are not a professional athlete or dancer—or, at least, not anymore. You're probably like our Granny, a "good full-figured woman" with bad knees. And a surefire way to end up with OA is the stress of carrying around 300 pounds!

If you are overweight, the excessive weight across your joints causes great wear and tear, especially in the "weight-bearing" joints. Areas like the knees, hips, and back are mainly responsible for supporting the bulk of your bulk. In these areas the cushion between the bones (the cartilage) has been worn down and destroyed, and your joints aren't happy about it. So what do they do? They scream. And this brings us to the symptoms of arthritis.

Of course, the main symptom is pain! It can be a deep, throbbing pain, or it can be sharp. Often, the pain becomes worse with continued use of the joint (notice how your knees hurt more the longer you stand or walk), and it gets better when you rest. But if the arthritis is severe, the pain can be constant. Cartilage itself has no nerve endings, so the cartilage isn't what's causing all the pain. So what causes the pain? The answer to that question goes to show how the cartilage (or its lack) is only part of the arthritis equation.

Once excess weight starts to wear down your "shock absorbers," the bone underneath the cartilage (that the cartilage is meant to protect) starts to erode in some places and abnormal bone grows in other places. What you end up with are bone "spurs." And they are as painful as they sound. Picture a spur on a cowboy's boot. Now picture that spur wedged in your joint. Ouch!

And that's not all. Pain from degenerative forms of arthritis also comes from the muscles around the joint. The muscles around your knees help to make your knees more stable and help to relieve some of the pressure from your body weight. When the joint becomes weak and diseased, the muscles are forced to work harder to stabilize the joints. When worked too hard, the muscles can begin to spasm and cause a significant amount of pain.

In addition to the pain, the inflammation of arthritis also causes swelling around the joint. And in addition to swelling, there's the formation of arthritic tissue.

Take a look at your knees. Do they look a little "chubby?" If you have arthritis, that "chubbiness" may not be extra fat (though it could be), and may not even be swelling (although it could be that as well!) If you've had arthritis for quite some time, it is possible that what you see is arthritic tissue (similar to scar tissue) that forms in response to the continuous injury done to the knee. And what I mean by "continuous injury" is that if you weigh 200, 250, or 300-plus pounds, with each step your knees must support that load, and, as a result, more damage occurs to the joints.

If you've ever had any type of chronic pain, you know how disabling it can be. Quite recently, I've developed muscular pain in my neck—it's not due to arthritis, and doesn't involve any real weight-bearing joints. But it does affect how far I can turn my head, how comfortably I can sleep, how quickly I can put on my shirt, and so on. It is awful.

Excuse me for interrupting, but if anyone has seen how big my sister's head is, they know that her neck is a major "weight-bearing" joint!

As I was saying, although this awful pain in my neck is due to bad posture and body mechanics, the stiffness that has resulted is like the chronic pain of arthritis. (I'm sure Stacy will tell us all very shortly about the role body mechanics play in arthritis!)

I've always thought I had a high tolerance for pain. I had my wisdom teeth taken out without being put to sleep and was off pain medicine within a week. I get really bad cramps that almost double me over and I endure them " like a champ" every month. But constant pain that doesn't go away is miserable and horrible and debilitating. And if there is any way I can avoid having this kind of pain in my joints, I'll do it!

So other than the pain, how else can your doctor diagnose your arthritis? After doing a complete history and physical exam, he or she will probably order some X-rays of the joints that are bothering you. What your doctor is really doing is making sure that the arthritis is not due to a "systemic" disease like rheumatoid arthritis or lupus. Systemic means that the disease is not limited to your sore knees or back but can affect other organs, like the lungs and liver in rheumatoid arthritis, or the skin and kidneys in lupus. The changes that occur with these systemic diseases look different on X-rays than the changes that occur with osteoarthritis and degenerative joint problems.

Once it's clear that there is nothing going on but a wearing down of your joints, your physician should tell you what you probably don't want to hear: you're too fat. There are several ways that you can deal with the info. You can be like my patient "Jane Doe" and deny, deny, deny. But this approach won't make the pain go away. Weight loss is a key step in the treatment of all types of arthritis, and there's no way around it if you want to feel better and stay that way.

My patients often tell me that losing weight is fine and good, but it takes time and they're in pain now. So what can be done? Arthritis can be partially caused by, and made worse by, poor body mechanics, such as poor posture. Take, for instance, arthritis of the lower back. The lower back carries a lot of your body weight, not only when you're standing but when you're sitting as well. When you have poor posture and your spine is humped and twisted over, this makes more problems for the joints in the back. The same is true with the knees and hips.

In response to pain, it's natural to change the way we move in order to lessen the pain and discomfort. That is why you've seen people with arthritis bent over in strange ways: their bodies are trying to get comfortable and compensate for the pain they are feeling. But this compensation actually makes things worse. So, for some people, the use of braces, canes, and walking devices help to take pressure off the joint and improve the posture.

Heat is also effective in easing the pain and stiffness of

arthritis, especially when used along with anti-inflammatory drugs like ibuprofen and aspirin. Acetaminophen (Tylenol®) is also used for pain control, but narcotic medicines (like Vicodin®, codeine, and Percocet®) should not be used, or if they are, they should be given only sparingly and for short periods of time. The reason is obvious. These medicines have addictive and habit-forming properties and should only be used as last resorts.

Exercise is one of the cornerstones of treating arthritis, and I'm not talking about the exercise needed to lose weight, which I'll come back to. Exercise therapy in arthritis is aimed toward helping the pain and the stiffness. Activities that focus on certain joints help to keep them flexible, and activity even helps to lubricate the cartilage that remains. So as you can see, stopping activity when you have arthritis is a bad thing to do. As painful as it is, you must keep the joints moving.

Besides helping to keep joints flexible, exercise builds up the muscles surrounding the diseased joint. Take the back for instance. If the muscles of the stomach and those surrounding the back are strengthened, then those muscles take on the task of supporting that area, and less pressure is placed on the bones of the back. Consider it giving your joints a vacation by letting the muscles do the work.

Yes, if you are arthritic you need exercise therapy. But the ultimate relief for painful joints—you guessed it—is weight loss. I know you don't want to hear me say it yet again, but it's unavoidable. Regardless of the type of arthritis you suffer from, if you are overweight or obese, you must lose weight.

> *The ultimate relief for painful joints—you guessed it—is weight loss.*

Understandably, it is a tough proposition. As my patient Jane said so well, "The heavier you get, the more your joints get worn down and the worse your arthritis." At the same time, the pain prevents you from exercising, so you gain more weight due to the inactivity. And the more weight you gain, the worse the arthritis. And so on and so on.

This cycle is hard to break, but you must break it if you are to find true relief from the arthritis. Even a weight loss of as little as ten pounds can translate into greatly relieved symptoms.

The treatment of last resort for arthritis is to go under the knife. Surgery can replace the knees or hips, and spinal surgery is an option for severe, disabling back degeneration. But the benefits of these surgeries are extremely limited unless the person first *loses weight*. If you think your body fat can wear down bone, trust me when I say that it can wear down a prosthetic joint as well.

Obese people have much worse outcomes than others when they undergo joint replacement surgery. Not only is the risk of the surgery greater (remember the lung and heart complications), but there is also a greatly increased risk of the wound not healing properly and more chance of infection. On top of that, all those pounds can cause the new mechanical joint to loosen and be displaced. This leads to more pain and more surgeries—obviously, not a good result. What's more, once a damaged joint is replaced, in order for you to fully recover use of the joint you must have extensive physical therapy. And that physical therapy includes—of course—*exercise*.

Now, decades later, our Granny O is "sixty-one" (she's claimed that age almost as long as I can remember!) and the years and the injuries have permanently damaged her joints.

Aside from the arthritis, she's in really good shape. But (though you'd never get her to admit it) the pain from her arthritis gets really bad. A lot of it is due to the natural aging process. But a lot of the damage—the heels, the knees, and, most important, the extra weight—began long ago, before she was actually, really, "sixty-one."

By itself, arthritis isn't fatal like cancer, diabetes, or heart disease. But it keeps millions of people from fully enjoying life, family, and friends. Those days in the park with your children or grandchildren only last a short time. You want to enjoy them actively, not stiffly and in pain from the park bench.

Part Three

The Path to Right Weight and Well-being

Chapter Nine   *Why Quick Fixes Rarely Fix*

I hope the journey we've been on together has been informative and enlightening. I also hope it may help you save a life—your own, or that of someone you love.

Maybe what you've read thus far has scared you enough by showing the impact of obesity on your health and even on your life span. Or maybe you've just learned one of the key messages of this book: to love and respect yourself. It follows that you will take good care of your body.

But the reality is that, like most of us, you've probably tried some of everything in your own personal quest for weight loss and may still be shopping for that miracle fix that will require little effort from you. Certainly, we all know people who get excited by miracle weight loss programs only to lose faith in them.

Well, here's where Teri can finally speak as the expert she thinks she is at everything. She has tried many of these methods, including some I hadn't heard about, so you can learn from her experiences as well as your own.

At seventeen, I packed my bags and headed off across the country to college. And what was there to meet me? My worst nightmare. The "freshman fifteen." These are the 15 (and sometimes20) pounds that inevitably follow the start of freshman year in college. No one, even Doc Stacy, is immune. The late nights studying, and midnight runs for Church's chicken, pizza, and Häagen Dazz™ ice cream set me up for that fifteen pound weight gain.

When I first gained those awful 15 pounds, I didn't get too worried. Because I had a plan. I was going on a "grapefruit and egg" diet. The promise was that I could lose up to 20 pounds in two weeks. How can you beat that? What's more, it had to be safe! I got it from my mother, who used it all the time, and next to my sister, she was the thinnest person I knew!

Here's what I ate:

Monday, Tuesday, Wednesday, Friday: grapefruit, boiled eggs, tomato, lettuce

Thursday: grapefruit, tomato, steak (all the steak I wanted!)

Saturday and Sunday: more grapefruit, boiled eggs, tomato

Did it work? You better believe it worked! It worked for a whole two weeks. And the minute I started back at my normal eating, the weight I lost—plus a couple of extra pounds—slipped back on. Diet failure number 1, but believe me, it wasn't to be the last.

Crash Diets

My sister is like most sisters battling the bulge. For most, crash diets are the first pick when the reality strikes you that your pants no longer fit. The *crash* in "crash diet" is defined as "marked by an intensive effort to produce or accomplish something quickly." So when you go on a crash diet, by definition you are trying to get fast results. But crash also has another meaning that I find more relevant to dieting: "to fail suddenly." This meaning describes pretty accurately what is going to happen when and if you try this method of weight loss.

There have been more crash diets in recent years than you can imagine. And believe me, there are many people making lots of money by preying on women's desperation and their erroneous desire for the "quick fix." In fact, each year Americans spend over $30 billion dollars (yes, that's billion with a *B)* on crash-diet books and pills and other false hopes about weight loss. Obviously, this means that there's a big diet industry that makes its profit by selling fixes that don't fix.

You've probably heard of, or even tried, some of the miracle diets that, in the end, "crashed." There have been cabbage soup diets, cayenne pepper diets, diets that require eating a dozen grapefruits a day, and diets that involve drinking large amounts of vinegar. The actual methods may be different, but all crash diets have some important common features.

All crash diets involve severe calorie restriction, which dooms them to failure. We all need calories to function. They're our fuel. If we take in more than we burn off, the extra calories will translate into extra weight. For a person who doesn't exercise or move around much, the right number of calories is body weight x 13. For the active person, it is body weight x 15.

For most of us, a caloric-restriction diet means eating less than a thousand or so calories a day, far less than we would take in from a normal diet. So the rapid weight loss that occurs is, for the most part, the result of fasting. And it's basically the fasting that makes you lose weight.

Yes, people who try these diets often get exactly what they

want from them—the initial loss of 5 to 10 pounds in a few days. But that immediate weight loss is mostly water weight, and will quickly come back once regular eating begins again.

Why will the weight return? When the body is faced with semi-starvation, its first reaction is to use the energy already stored in the body and that is immediately available. This energy does not come from fat. It comes from a substance called "glycogen." Glycogen is a carbohydrate stored in the liver and muscles. It is bound to water in a solution (this is how it is stored). So when the body breaks the glycogen down, it sheds a lot of water. That's why you lose weight by losing body water.

Incidentally, the body also breaks down muscle when it uses glycogen, which is not good for your long-term weight loss or health. So starvation diets cause you to lose almost no fat from the places that count (places like the abdomen, where excess fat is dangerous to your health).

Not only are these diets dangerous if you stay on them for any length of time, but, luckily, the physical side effects alone make it impossible for most people to tolerate crash diets for long. The physical side effects of a restrictive diet can include:

- Weakness
- Lightheadedness
- Complete lack of energy that accompanies fasting

These symptoms are your body's way of telling you that something isn't right. And my advice is for you to listen. Severe calorie restriction can be especially unpleasant and dangerous if you (like most obese individuals) have other health problems, such as undiagnosed heart disease or diabetes.

Now I want be more specific by looking closely at a few of the more famous fad diets.

Take the cabbage soup diet. It is marketed to suggest that cabbage soup contains some yet-to-be-named ingredient that boosts metabolism and burns fat. This diet requires eating cabbage soup several times a day, which, even if you happen to love cabbage, will soon become unbearable. As for calories, you are limited to approximately 900 calories a day, which is a severe limitation. The truth is that cabbage does not contain any magical properties. The reason you lose weight is because you are restricting calories, which would happen with or without the cabbage soup.

The same is true of the grapefruit diet, which began as "the Hollywood diet" in the 1930s. The marketing claim is that grapefruit has a substance that makes you burn calories and lose weight. As with the cabbage diet, the grapefruit works: it allows you to lose weight and lose it fast. But again, it's the extreme calorie restriction that accounts for the initial weight loss. No one sticks to these diets, in part because of the physical symptoms that come from fasting and in part from boredom. After a while, a person just gets a craving for anything other than cabbage or grapefruit.

The marketers of each new crash diet will try to convince you that their formula is "the one," but these diets all are nutritionally unbalanced and the chance of long-term success is virtually zero.

The marketers of each new crash diet will try to convince you that their formula is "the one," but these diets all are nutritionally unbalanced and the chance of long-term success is virtually zero. Let me explain another thing that happens when you're on a crash diet. Crash diets reduce calories to such low levels that the body goes into a "starvation mode." In that mode, the body hangs on to every calorie you take in, which makes it very hard to actually burn fat. In that way, the initial weight loss can turn into weight gain. These fad diets also cause extreme hunger and promote powerful food cravings. That means, when you do return to your ordinary diet, you will inevitably overeat in response to the starvation. And as you know, that can be as bad for your body as starving it.

Another common feature of these make-believe diets is that they don't include an exercise plan. There is a reason for that, of course. On the few calories these diets allow, you wouldn't have the energy or strength to exercise.

Finally, such diets don't ask you to think about the behaviors responsible for obesity or teach you new and better behaviors to replace them. By "behaviors," I mean things like:

- How much food you put on your plate and the plates of your loved ones
- How healthy the meals you prepare are
- Whether or not you get enough physical activity

So it doesn't matter what type of packaging these crash diets come in. Don't get fooled by the promises of miracle weight loss or by the sophisticated and colorful gimmicks. These diets deprive you of healthy nourishment and sidetrack you from your real goal:

a healthy and realistic plan to lose weight. So to make a long story short, if it sounds too good to be true, it is. Just say no.

Over-the-counter Diet Pills

In the spring of 1993, I discovered a brand new truth. Tired of crash diets and steadily gaining weight, I still needed to find something to help me keep off the excess pounds. My new truth was Dexatrim®, and I thought I had the magical fix. I took one tablet a day, and I swear to God I never got hungry! This stuff was the real goods. I mean, I had to schedule when I would eat, because if I waited until I was hungry, I wouldn't eat at all.

The pounds came off. The compliments came rushing in. And again, I was caught—on Dexatrim®, and on the compliments. But there was one problem. The directions on the box said that it was dangerous to use the pills for more than twenty-one days. So at the end of three weeks I put the pills away. My plan was to wait out the allotted time before starting back on the tablets again.

As soon as I stopped taking them, I was ravenous! So I gained a few pounds back. But by then the waiting period was over and I went right back on the Dexatrim™ plan. But this time, to my great disappointment, the pills didn't work. I took them and was still hungry.

What I found out was that after a certain amount of time, the pills become less effective and my body needed higher doses of the drug to regulate hunger. At the same time, I needed the pills because, as I discovered, the drug takes away the body's own ability to regulate hunger. I could see where that was going, so I stopped taking Dexatrin® although I didn't stop looking for a miracle fix.

I was never trained in marketing, but even I can see the beauty in placing diet pills near the junk food and soda aisles of the supermarkets. The arrangement is a way of reinforcing the myth that if you take pills, it doesn't matter what you eat and it doesn't matter if you keep up all your old bad eating habits, such as dependence on too much sugar and too much fat.

During the 1980s when diet pills really skyrocketed in popularity, America seemed to be all about overindulgence—in spending, in fashion, and, yes, in food as well. And the answer was as easy as a trip to the market. Dexatrim® and Acutrim® were the most well-known and popular over-the-counter diet pills. Both worked in the same way. Until the early '90s, they both contained a drug called "phenylpropanolamine," which is an appetite suppressant. (Phenylpropanolamine, or PPA, is also found in over-the-counter cough and cold medicines.)

There were several problems with the use of PPA in weight loss drugs. As the package warning label stated, there could be serious side effects in people who have heart disease or high blood pressure (or even a family history of heart disease), diabetes, strokes, or seizures. This is scary, because the drug is bought, obviously, by people with weight problems who are likely to have those illnesses, even if they are undiagnosed.

PPA was taken off the market in the early 1990s because it was found that people taking these drugs had higher rates of a particular type of stroke that involved bleeding in the brain. This condition, called "hemorrhagic" stroke, is serious and often fatal.

Don't think that once PPA was pulled off the market over-the-counter diet pills became safe. And don't think for one minute that the recall of PPA ended the over-the-counter diet pill craze. It didn't. The current versions of these diet pills not only suppress your appetite, but they also increase your metabolism. And the drug they use to do this is considered by most health professionals to be even more dangerous than the PPA it replaced. The new versions contain ephedra, an "herbal" supplement that speeds up metabolism. In fact, it really is "speed," a type of amphetamine. It's also a very risky drug to take, as I'll explain in more detail below.

Besides containing ephedra, most over-the-counter weight loss drugs and appetite suppressants also contain caffeine as part of the formula, supposedly to boost metabolism and energy. They also pose risks such as high blood pressure, strokes, and sudden death, especially in people (like those who are obese) who have underlying medical problems. The warning label, just like that of PPA in the 1990s, cautions against the use of caffeine if you or your family has a history of high blood pressure, heart disease, kidney disease, or stroke. What black person do you know who doesn't have any of these illnesses or doesn't have a family member who does? The fact is that the very people the drug is marketed to are the ones for whom the drugs are most dangerous.

The bottom line? Over-the-counter drugs don't work in the long term, and they can be very dangerous to your health. You can develop a tolerance to them (just like the illegal speed), so that higher and higher doses are needed to deliver the same effects. Such a pattern doesn't address the true issues of obesity, such as changing your eating and exercise habits.

A quick trip to the local grocery store will reveal other weight loss tools that don't fall under the "drug" category. There is an infinite supply of diet drinks and shakes that promise rapid results. The most popular at one time was Slim-Fast™. Their plan involves drinking a shake for breakfast and lunch, then eating a "sensible" dinner. In the medical community, this is known as "replacement" therapy, meaning that the diet shake is used to replace a meal. Therefore, the drink is supposed to provide all the necessary nutrients and energy that you need throughout the day. Although diet replacement programs like these drink diets have become more sophisticated in their marketing and advertising, when they are broken down, one core truth is revealed: the real cause of the weight loss is starvation.

Eating one meal a day will lead to weight loss initially, no matter what you drink for breakfast and lunch. But the key word here is "initially." Soon your body will catch on and go into "starvation mode." Your metabolism will slow down, and your calories will be stored away instead of burned off, making it harder to lose weight. That's why most people who use this type of plan hit a "wall" after losing that first five to seven pounds.

Anything that requires starvation in order to work actually works against your health goals in the long run.

Even more important, without exercise, you cannot achieve healthy weight loss, and in order to exercise, you need fuel. So anything that requires starvation in order to work actually works against your health goals in the long run.

There is still another common scenario with meal replacement diets. That "sensible" meal you are supposed to have in the evening? Well, after starving yourself all day, you are more likely to eat everything in sight than to be "sensible." Food restriction usually produces very powerful food cravings, which can sabotage any weight loss plan.

There is some evidence that meal replacement can help. The key is not to use the shakes in place of solid food.

Laxatives and Diuretics

Appetite suppressants and meal-replacement shakes are not the only over-the-counter tricks used when people try to confront their obesity. Laxatives have also been used in high doses in order to prevent food from being absorbed in the stomach. This is a bad idea in many ways. Besides causing you to spend a lot of time on the toilet, laxatives, and the diarrhea that follows their use, can cause an imbalance of electrolytes (such as potassium) and nutrients. This imbalance is dangerous to the heart and can even result in sudden death.

If you have diabetes and are taking laxatives to control your weight, the results can also be hazardous by causing extremes in your blood sugar, which is difficult to control.

People with a yen for quick-fix weight loss also use diuretics, or "water pills." But obviously the only thing you lose with a water pill is water, not fat. And the strongest diuretics, which are prescription only, can cause dehydration, kidney problems, and electrolyte imbalance (very low potassium levels). Again, diuretics are an ineffective and dangerous way to lose weight. Don't use them.

Prescription Drugs

After my diet pill debacle, I was still looking for that next big thing. And I thought I'd found it with Fen-Phen®. It had just come on the market and was supposed to be a miracle. I wanted it. I asked for it. To my disappointment, my doctor wouldn't prescribe it, on the grounds that I wasn't heavy enough!

My disappointment only got worse as I started hearing and seeing just how well Fen-Phen® worked. At the time, I thought, of all of the doctors out there who will prescribe weight loss drugs left and right, why do I have the one who follows the rules!

Prescription medications for obesity began to gain popularity in the early '90s with the release of the weight loss drug Fen-Phen®. Fen-Phen® is (or should I say was) a combination of two drugs, dexfenfluramine (also known as Redux®) a stimulant medication that causes a decrease in appetite, and fenfluramine (whose trade name is Pondimin®), which acts on a certain chemical in the brain (serotonin) to make you feel full more quickly.

Fen-Phen®, as the combination of drugs is called, was an effective weight loss drug for most people. After a while, however, we saw that people who took the drug longer than, say, six months, developed a serious and often fatal disease called *primary pulmonary hypertension*. Primary pulmonary hypertension (also called PPH) is a rare, deadly disease that affects the blood vessels in the lungs. Death results within four to five years of the diagnosis in about half of those who contract the disease. PPH is almost never seen in people who have not taken fenfluramine or dexfenfluramine, either alone or in combination.

Further, we learned that abnormalities of the heart valves were becoming incredibly common in those who took the drugs. Eventually, as everyone who has not been living in a cave over the past decade knows, Fen-Phen® was taken off the market and its makers are still up to their ears in lawsuits. But we haven't quite seen the last of these types of drugs, so stay tuned.

Natural Remedies

So no Fen-Phen® for me. But just about the same time a new wonder drug came out that claimed to increase metabolism, build muscle, and get people in shape really fast. This new drug was called "herbal fen-phen," and was billed as "all natural." That would make it safe, right?

Wrong! "Herbal" and "all natural" does not equal "safe." To be sure, there *are* useful herbal medicines, though I'm in the minority of doctors who believe that. In fact, I often prescribe them, along with standard "Western" medicines, because they can contribute to the health and well-being of my patients.

That being said, there are weight loss drugs like herbal fen-phen that are not only useless but also positively harmful. Too many black women have been hoodwinked into buying these drugs by a multibillion-dollar industry that has preyed upon our fears, insecurities, and ignorance. Let me give you a rundown on some of these.

Like the prescription Fen-Phen® that was taken off the market by the FDA, the herbal version can be dangerous. Herbal fen-phen is a combination of two substances: St. John's Wort and ephedra. St. John's Wort is an herbal product that has some mild anti-depressant activity. It presumably duplicates the supposed anti-depressant effects of the drug fenfluramine, though, as it turned out, fenfluramine actually has no anti-depressant properties. The herbal version of Fen-Phen® also includes ephedra, a non-prescription stimulant drug, similar to amphetamines, that decreases appetite.

But the fact is that substances that appear "safe" can sometimes actually cause harm. Ephedra (a substitute for the drug dexfenfluramine in the prescription version) though it doesn't cause PPH or heart valve problems as dexfenfluamine does, can cause heart attacks, strokes, and abnormalities in the way your heart beats. That's why it is associated with cases of sudden death in young, previously healthy patients.

Women in our community also use other "natural" herbal drugs containing caffeine, kola nut, guarana, and of course, ephedra as stimulants that are intended to suppress appetite. Ma huang is another substance to be wary of. Teenagers use it as a "party drug," under the name "herbal ecstasy." It is simply another variation of very potent amphetamines, or speed. And it is equally dangerous.

Some herbal medicines marketed as treatments for obesity, although they don't do any harm, as the stimulant medications do, also don't do much good. Chromium picolinate is one such drug. The makers claim that it works by strengthening metabolism and decreasing your appetite. But the only "decreasing" we can be sure of is that it decreases the size of your wallet.

Chitosan is a natural remedy used for weight loss that includes a substance called "chitin." Chitin is a carbohydrate found in the outer skeleton of shrimp, crab, and shellfish. It is supposed to block the absorption of fat from the foods you eat. Does it work? As you'd guess, companies that market trade versions of chitosan claim that it does, but the medical community is not so sure. What is for sure is that the "secret" to weight loss and a healthy body will never be found in a pill or powder.

The "secret" to weight loss and a healthy body will never be found in a pill or powder.

One last problem with herbal medicine: because herbal drugs are not monitored by the Food and Drug Administration (the FDA), there is no standard dose or universal recommendation as to how much you can take safely. Also, the amount of drug varies from brand to brand and even from bottle to bottle within the same brand. So what you buy on Monday may not contain the same ingredients as what you buy on Friday. Five times more or less of an herbal supplement may not make much difference if the ingredients are harmless. But if they're dangerous, like ephedra or other stimulants, an increased dosage could be deadly.

So don't trust a drug just because it is labeled "natural" or "safe." Read the label and talk to your doctor. Then you can see for yourself if it contains ingredients you know aren't safe. And remember, if you have high blood pressure, diabetes, or other forms of heart disease (as many overweight and obese women do) these herbal substances can be particularly dangerous.

The root causes of obesity are lack of physical activity and poor eating choices.

The root causes of obesity are lack of physical activity and poor eating choices. That means that, yes, weight loss requires work on your part. That work begins when you understand that the ultimate goal of weight loss is to live a long and healthy life, free of disease. You can't reach that goal by sitting on a couch munching chips, or by going out and ordering fast food, or by falling victim to the newest quick-fix diet craze. In the long run, nothing will work (prescription drug or non-prescription) unless you exercise and eat a healthy diet.

I worked my way through lots of diet and weight loss fads, and came away an expert on what doesn't work. I also happen to be an information junkie and a hypochondriac. If there is a disease to be gotten, I'm sure I have it. And if there is an injury to happen, I'm sure it will happen to me. So before I jumped on the ephedra craze, I got on the computer and did some research. And being in the news business, I came across story after story of people who had medical complications after taking ephedra-based products. That was enough to scare me away from ephedra permanently!

But even though I was too scared to take it, I was still attracted to the idea that herbal or prescription Fen-Phen®, or some other pill I could pop, could be the magic solution to my weight problems. Yeah, nothing down and nothing to pay.

I toyed with the "what ifs." What if I took the drug and miraculously lost all of the weight I wanted to lose, without any effort? Wouldn't that solve all of my problems? Just think, I'd never have to diet or exercise again. I imagined I was merely one tablet away—only fear was holding me back. Lucky for me, fear won.

Chapter Ten   *What Is a Healthy Diet?*

Now I think you're ready to start working, so here is where all that you've read so far gets put into action. My aim isn't to offer a new miracle diet. Instead, it's to offer some medical advice and a little common sense about the subject of losing weight. As always, losing weight and keeping it lost is about choices, choices made on the basis of accurate knowledge and genuine understanding and commitment. Being overweight and obese are medical conditions that need treatment, and the right choices mean effective treatment.

I wish Stacy wouldn't say "treatment" when she's talking about how to lose weight. For me the word "treatment" brings up images of illness and death and such bad stuff. And if you're like me, hardly ever sick and in a state of good overall health, the word "treatment" just doesn't feel right. So I'm officially renaming this chapter. From now on, I'll refer to it only as the "do the damned thang" chapter. With the emphasis on DO. So let's get started.

The first step in any weight loss program is a trip to the doctor. If you do not like the one you have, find another one. It always amazes me how people, especially women, will stay with a physician whom they don't like, who doesn't listen, and who is not doing an appropriate job.

Not only should your physician help to fine-tune an exercise and diet plan for you, but also you must be evaluated for diseases such as diabetes and heart disease that may have previously been undiagnosed. Heart disease can dangerously complicate any exercise program. The time to discover you have high blood pressure or blocked arteries is not on a treadmill at the gym, when it may be too late. You and your doctor can also calculate your Body Mass Index (or BMI), and figure out what is a realistic weight goal for you. Lab tests such as cholesterol (taken on an empty stomach) and thyroid tests, should also be done, as well as a good physical exam. Other tests may be necessary if you are older or already have heart disease, diabetes, or risk factors that make you more likely to have these illnesses.

So once you've seen your doctor, and have been given the green light to start a diet and exercise program, what's next? Well, the biggest issue you have to face is likely to be food. Food is such a large part of our everyday lives. We think about it constantly, and our social events are centered around it (when you meet a friend, where do you go? For dinner or drinks, of course.) But the key thing to remember is that food is good. You need it to live and to be healthy. So the issue is not with food itself, but with food choices.

The food choices you make from day to day are your diet. So your first job is to make the choices that make up a "balanced diet." Naturally, that will vary from person to person. It has also been complicated somewhat by changes in expert thinking on the subject. Even today, there are different views held within the medical community.

But on several key points all knowledgeable people do agree. A balanced diet is generally made up of several groups of food, the main ones being carbohydrates and protein. You need both to stay healthy, but surprisingly, most people really have no idea what a carbohydrate is or why protein is so important. Well, today is your lucky day, because I'm about to tell you.

Carbohydrates

Let's start with carbohydrates. The current trend is to avoid carbohydrates at all costs. However, once you learn what a carbohydrate really is, you'll see why avoiding them completely is not a good idea.

A carbohydrate is a compound produced when plants are exposed to sunlight (a process called "photosynthesis"). Because of this, foods that are derived from plants are high in carbohydrates. These include foods such as fruits, vegetables, grains, seeds, and nuts. Sugar, which is derived from the plant sugar cane, is also a source of carbohydrates.

The reason why carbs are so important to a healthy diet is that the cells of the body mainly run on glucose, which is a sugar molecule your body uses to make energy. When you eat carbs, your body breaks them down into glucose, which your body uses as energy.

Because carbohydrates equal energy, you can see why they are such a necessary part of a healthy diet. However, not all carbohydrates are created equal. As I'll explain in a moment, there are serious nutritional differences between a donut and a piece of whole-grain bread, or between white rice and brown rice. Recognizing those differences is an important part of a healthy diet.

Protein

After carbohydrates, the next major food group that's essential to every diet is protein. Protein is a molecule, which, when broken down, becomes an amino acid. Proteins are not typically used for energy by the body. They are used to make new cells, to produce hormones and enzymes, and to maintain the tissues in your body. Unlike carbohydrates and fat, proteins aren't stored by your body when you eat more than you need, so you need a constant supply.

You can get protein from animal products such as fish, poultry, and beef, and from plant products such as veggies. While animal protein generally contains all the amino acids needed for the body, plant protein is often "incomplete," so you cannot get the full variety of amino acids in one food. This doesn't mean everyone has to eat meat. It simply means that if you are vegetarian, you must eat a variety of plant products in order to get all the essential amino acids your body needs. How much protein you need each day differs from person to person, but the standard requirement is approximately 1 to 1.2 grams of protein (animal or plant) each day for each kilogram of your body weight.

Fats and Oils

The last major food group is fats and oils (oils are just fats that are liquid at room temperature). Yes, even fat is a vital part of a healthy diet. It insulates your body, helps you use such vitamins as vitamins A and E, helps build and maintain nerve cells, and makes hormones like testosterone.

The key to fat, as to most things in life, is that you must limit the amount and pay attention to the type of fat you eat.

Oh yeah, you also need fat to make breasts, hips, and all those other curves. Further, as you will soon see, there are good fats that even help to keep your heart healthy.

The key to fat, as to most things in life, is that you must limit the amount and pay attention to the type of fat you eat. Too much of the wrong kind of fat is linked to diabetes, heart disease, and cancer.

Not all fats are bad. To make things simple, the foods to avoid are foods high in "saturated fats." Butter, that rich, creamy, yellow bundle of happiness that is a major food group in parts of the South, is almost completely made of saturated fat. That is why it clogs up your arteries and widens your hips. Meats can also have high levels of saturated fat, while carbohydrates typically have very low levels.

To make things simple, the foods to avoid are foods high in "saturated fats."

There are two other types of fat to keep in mind. Monounsaturated fats, such as olive oil, for example, lower cholesterol and so is good for your heart. Nuts, seeds, and flaxseed oil, all monounsaturated, are on the "good" list.

Polyunsaturated fats can also be good for you, especially if they contain omega-3 oils. Omega-3 fats are found in fish and in soybean and canola oils. Like monounsaturated fats, they lower LDL and triglyceride levels and thus benefit the heart.

But polyunsaturated vegetable oils can mean trouble, and the more processed the oil is, the worse it is for you.

The most dangerous fats are called *trans fats*, and you will find them in partially hydrogenated vegetable oil, most margarines, most commercial baked goods, and deep-fried chips.

Dietary Fats

Type of Fat	Main Source	State at Room Temperature	Effect on Cholesterol
Monounsaturated	Olives; olive oil, canola oil, peanut oil; cashews, almonds, peanuts, and most other nuts; avocados	Liquid	Lowers LDL; raises HDL
Polyunsaturated	Corn, soybean, safflower, and cottonseed oils; fish	Liquid	Lowers LDL; raises HDL
Saturated	Whole milk, butter, cheese, and ice cream; red meat; chocolate; coconuts, coconut milk, and coconut oil	Solid	Raises both LDL and HDL
Trans	Most margarines; vegetable shortening; partially hydrogenated vegetable oil; deep-fried chips; many fast foods; most commercial baked goods	Solid or semi-solid	Raises LDL

The absolute worst fats are the "partially hydrogenated" oils, such as margarine. Trans fats raise LDL (bad cholesterol) levels, and are heavy in calories, (about 130 calories a tablespoon).

To sum up, if we can say that monounsaturated and polyunsaturated fats are "good" fats, and partially hydrogenated fats and saturated fats are "bad," then trans fats are the "ugly." Trans fat are found in animal products, and they are also made synthetically when food processors harden the fat to make it more like butter. These "partially hydrogenated fats," such as margarine, are the worst trans fats of all, but all trans fats raise LDL levels (bad cholesterol) and significantly add to your risk of heart disease and stroke.

The FDA feels that limiting the amount of trans fat is so important to public health that, by the time you read this, manufacturers of food products will be required to state the amount of trans fat contained in the foods you eat. So far, there has not been a "safe" level established, but the goal is to eat as little of it as possible. So how do you know which foods have which types of fat? Simple. You must read the food label. Make this a new good habit.

Balancing Your Diet

So now we know what a carbohydrate is and what proteins do, and that fats are a necessary part of everyone's diet. How much of each do you need? Again, there is no one correct answer.

Since the 1950s, medical and nutrition "experts" have used the USDA (U.S. Department of Agriculture) food pyramid as the model for a balanced diet. To this day, it is still printed on the label of most food products. The USDA food pyramid recommends:

- 6 to 11 servings of bread, rice, cereal, or pasta
- 2 to 4 servings of fruit
- 3 to 5 servings of vegetables
- 2 to 3 servings of meat, fish, eggs, beans, or nuts
- sparing use of fats and oils

How many servings you eat each day depends on how many calories a day you consume. For example, if you are on a 2,200 calorie eating plan, you would consume the higher number of servings each day, and if you were dieting to lose weight, you would stick to the lower number of servings from each group. On this traditional plan, you would end up having around 60 percent of your calories from carbohydrates, 20 percent from protein, and 20 percent from fats.

So is the USDA food pyramid a good model for you? Yes and no. Admittedly, experts disagree, but I can tell you what I think is useful about the USDA's food pyramid, and then we'll touch on what I think isn't reliable advice today.

The pyramid encourages five or more portions of fruits and vegetables each day. Veggies are good for the heart and good at preventing many forms of cancer, and, as we've seen in the earlier chapters, veggies help to lower cholesterol and prevent diabetes. The traditional food pyramid also recommends consuming only small amounts of fat, which is generally considered a wise thing to do.

However, there are recommendations in the USDA food pyramid that could actually hinder your weight loss goals. The biggest issue I have with the food pyramid is that it wrongly assumes that all of us are chemically and metabolically the same. We are not. Some of our bodies are genetically wired to do quite well with larger amounts of carbohydrates, some of us do better on vegetarian plans, some of us should eliminate dairy or eat more protein. The USDA pyramid supposes that "one size fits all" for diet and nutrition. It couldn't be more wrong.

Good and Bad Carbs

Another issue I have with the pyramid is that it fails to distinguish between "good" carbohydrates and "bad" carbohydrates. That's a critical omission, in my view, since people's ignorance about carbs is at the heart of America's obesity problem.

Remember that "carbohydrate" is a term that describes any food produced by plants. This means that good ol' broccoli is a carbohydrate, but so is a Krispy Krème™ donut. Common sense will tell you that one is infinitely better for you (if you don't know which one, we have some serious work to do). But the traditional food pyramid does nothing to separate one from the other, so your veggie source of carbs could consist of French fries or potato chips, or maybe a hamburger bun, a couple of donuts, and a few helpings of fried rice to fulfill your bread/rice/cereal requirement. A diet such as this will inevitably lead to obesity, heart disease, and diabetes.

Happily, there are a few general guidelines that may help you quickly identify the good from the not-so-good food choice. Since this is a book for women of color, it should be easy for you to remember that the color of the food can usually help you to make better food choices. The more colorful the food, the more likely it is to contain all the natural chemicals and antioxidants that protect against disease. So when it comes to carbohydrates, white is "bad" because it usually means the food has been highly processed and refined.

I recommend that you pick breads, cereals, and grains that have color, such as whole grains, bran, rye breads, brown rice and pasta, and whole wheat. As for vegetables, green, red, purple, and orange are just doing everything they can to grab your attention and get you to snatch them out of the produce section and take them home. White veggies, like potatoes, should be placed on the "special occasion" list and should not be part of your daily diet plan.

The more colorful the food, the more likely it is to contain all the natural chemicals and antioxidants that protect against disease.

Why some carbohydrates are better for you than others is thought to have something to do with their glycemic index. This is a term we commonly run into in food plans for people with diabetes, but it also explains why carbohydrates have been given such a bad rap. The glycemic index indicates how fast the body breaks a carbohydrate down into glucose (or sugar). A food with a very high glycemic index is quickly broken down to glucose and your blood sugar level will rapidly go up. When blood sugar levels go up, insulin levels go up as well in order to clear the sugar from the bloodstream. Insulin is a hormone with many functions, and one of those functions is to increase fat storage.

So the glycemic index potentially explains why we get so fat when we eat certain foods. Table sugar and refined, processed carbohydrates (like chips, donuts, white breads) have a very high glycemic index. So do white potatoes. Foods with a low glycemic index are broken down by the body more slowly, so blood sugar levels rise over time and, therefore, you don't see the big surge of insulin. This is a good thing (less insulin surge means less fat storage). Foods such as broccoli, strawberries, green beans, grapefruit, spinach, rye bread, and oatmeal (the list goes on) have a lower glycemic index. (And did you notice that all these foods have color?)

Another weakness of the food pyramid is that it doesn't address fiber. The fiber content of a particular food helps determine the glycemic index. It does this by shielding the carbohydrates you eat from immediate digestion,

Fiber is the non-digestible part of plants. We find it in veggies, nuts, beans, and unrefined grain. It is a carbohydrate, but it isn't digested quickly, so it does not raise blood sugar levels. Not only does fiber break down slowly, but it also causes other carbohydrates to digest more slowly.

Another benefit of fiber is that it binds to the cholesterol in your stomach, and then helps your body get rid of it—which means it helps lower your cholesterol levels.

Still another reason fiber should be a big part of your diet is that it eliminates toxins and poisons in the intestines that are created by bacteria. (Don't be freaked out, bacteria are a natural part of the normal intestine.)

Last, but not least, fiber makes you feel really full, so you eat less because your brain turns off the "hungry" signal earlier. To a dieter, fiber can be a girl's best friend.

The two big reasons why you should not be misled by the USDA food pyramid are:

- The pyramid fails to distinguish between good and bad carbohydrates,

- The pyramid does not take into account that there are good and bad fats. (Higher levels of fat may actually be good for your health if it's the right fat—for example, olive oil instead of Crisco.)

High Protein Diets

You have probably heard of several diet plans that say that high protein, high fat, low carbohydrate is the way to go. While the USDA pyramid has approximately 60 percent of calories coming from carbohydrates and 20 percent from protein, these high protein plans have 40 and sometimes 50 percent protein and 20 to 30 percent carbohydrates. They also have over 30 percent of calories coming from fat. So you see, there is a major difference in thinking within the medical and nutritional communities.

High protein diets are very much a fad today. They push protein and discourage carbs. It's that old familiar story: the failure to distinguish between good carbs and bad carbs.

There are two reasons why some health professionals advocate such low cabohydrate/high protein diets as the Atkins Diet, The Zone, or Protein Power. First, the professionals note that since the widespread use of the USDA food pyramid, America has gotten fatter and fatter. Clearly, the pyramid diet plan isn't working, so they turn to the high protein diet.

Another reason some people advocate such diets is the belief that eating high protein diets is "in our genes" because many thousands of years ago (caveman times), humans ate diets primarily consisting of the meat they hunted and killed.

In my own opinion (and I urge you to form your own), the "protein pushers" are partially correct. Americans have gotten bigger and bigger on high carbohydrate diets, but the real reason may be not that carbohydrates make us fat but that the *wrong* carbohydrates do.

People aren't getting fatter because they are eating too much broccoli and brown rice. The problem is French fries and Doritos—that is, bad fat and processed, refined sugar.

As to whether meat-eating is molded into our genes, well, maybe, but we still do make choices. People did eat a lot of meat when they were hunters, and until recent times, because they worked hard enough physically to work off the calories. But today more and more people are living sedentary lives. We're not out hunting buffalos, but sitting on the sofa, getting up only to go to the fridge or order take-out.

Our lack of physical activity gets worse and worse as technology makes things more convenient. Now everything is at our fingertips, and as simple as a click of the mouse. And be totally honest: How many times have you watched the same television channel all day because you could not find the remote? Exactly. We aren't even willing to walk a few steps to the TV anymore, much less go out and kill food. So although our ancestors had different diets than we do today, they also had different lifestyles to support their diets.

The important reason people love these high protein diets is that they lose weight very quickly at the beginning of the program. The reason that happens is that your body uses glucose (sugar) for energy. When you drastically cut down carbs, your body tries to use protein and fat for energy. It's very hard work for the body to pull energy out of these substances, and a lot of water is produced in the process (water is a by-product of metabolism or energy production).

Simply put, you pee a lot. So much so that the initial five to seven pounds lost on these high protein diets is water weight and the loss, in most cases, is only temporary.

Another reason people love these diets is that they allow, even encourage, high quantities of meat and fat. That's certainly an attraction for meat eaters, but remind yourself: lots of meat means a lot of extra fat and cholesterol. So while you may be losing weight, you may also be hurting your heart.

Veggies and grains (carbohydrates) are in short supply on many of these diets. Again, that's bad news for your health, since veggies and grains help lower the risk of cancer and heart disease.

Still another problem with low-carb diets is that, when your body burns things other than sugar for food, ketosis develops. Ketosis is an abnormal state also seen as a response to starvation. It can be harmful to the kidneys, and it can also make you feel lousy, giving you headaches, fatigue, nausea, dizziness, and bad breath.

For people who are diabetic, these very high protein diets carry special dangers, and they should be tried only with your doctor's approval and supervision.

Of course, you do need protein in your diet every day (remember that you cannot store it). A safe amount of protein for the average person is 0.8–1.0 grams for every kilogram of body weight each day. Remember that you need protein every day to prevent your body from digesting its own muscle mass.

To sum up, in the choice between the USDA high carbohydrate plan and the very high protein/low carbohydrate plans, my best advice is that you stay somewhere in the middle. Certainly, cut down on processed, refined kinds of carbohydrates. But the very high protein recommendations are too high for the average person. So I generally advise a "modified food pyramid":

- Carbohydrates to make up no more than 50 percent of daily calories.
- Protein to make up 25-30 percent of total calories
- Protein to come from animal and plant sources.
- Fat to make up no more than 30 percent of your diet. Many experts recommend as low as 10%.

I also strongly recommend that you buy a scale and a measuring cup, and use these tools to weigh out serving sizes. Eventually, you will get so good at identifying a real serving size that you will be able to do it just by looking.

Talk with your doctor about a food plan that fits your health history and your lifestyle. If your doctor isn't willing, or able, to get you started, find a new doctor.

So How Much?

I wish the weight problem we African Americans have could be solved simply by changing the types of food we eat. But in fact, we must also take a hard look at how much we eat. Too many of us honestly believe that a serving is whatever you can fit on your plate. It isn't.

Benjamin Franklin stated over three hundred years ago: " To lengthen thy life, lessen thy meals." That was good advice then, and it's good advice now. Even with all the advances that have been made in the science of obesity, even considering all the research in insulin resistance and hormones, the ultimate root of the problem was known three hundred years ago.

Our ignoring Franklin's advice is one of the reasons for the "supersizing of America." If you have ever eaten out in any other country, your first reaction when the meal was brought was probably a mixture of surprise, curiosity, and anger. Surprise at how small the portions were, curiosity because you wondered where the rest of it was and when they were going to bring it, and, finally, anger when you discovered that there was no more coming and you couldn't get your money back. Visitors to the United States are equally shocked to see the enormous amounts of food that are served to them.

We simply have a problem with knowing what a serving size is and how much a portion is supposed to be. Even foods that are adopted from other countries, bagels or croissants, for example, have grown to unbelievable sizes. The bagel of today is almost twice the size of a bagel from the 1960s. Our croissants are bigger and have one hundred more calories than the French croissant. And those blueberry muffins you scarf down with your coffee each morning? They started off as 1 ounce many years ago, but the current muffin weighs in at 6 to 8 ounces! That's four times the size it should be.

The increase in size is driven by Americans demand for "supersized" items. This shows us something about the eating habits of the American public: We do not have a clue! We eat whatever can be piled on a plate or fit into our line of vision, regardless of the number of actual servings we devour. Effective health and weight loss involves knowing and understanding what a real portion is. Don't be mad when I tell you. It's not the end of the world (but it is the beginning of good health!).

The USDA has established standard serving sizes for all types of food. Examples: an apple that is roughly the size of your fist is considered one serving of fruit. No problem there, but how about this: a serving of cheese weighs 1 ounce, which is the size of a woman's thumb. Think how many servings of cheese are on a pizza or in a pot of macaroni and cheese.

For carbs, one serving is a slice of bread, or half a cup of pasta, or half a cup of rice. A serving of rice is about the size of a golf ball. Makes you go "hmmmm," doesn't it?

And what about meat? A serving of meat is a 1-ounce piece of steak, or 2 ounces of cooked lean meat such as chicken or fish. A serving of meat is approximately the size of the palm of your hand.

As for veggies, one serving is half a cup of string beans or broccoli. But I would guess that people do not get obese by eating too much lettuce or too many carrots. (Have you ever seen a 300-pound rabbit?)

What it boils down to is that a plate of food in the typical American-style restaurant gives you two to three servings. That would be fine if you just divided up the plate and ate some for breakfast, some for lunch, and the rest for dinner. Taken in at one meal, such a serving is much too big.

Reading the Label

Sticking to healthy portion sizes is half the battle. You also need to read labels and see how much of each product makes up a serving. Even when you are eating food that you'd do better to avoid altogether, like chips, cookies, or other junk foods, a serving is not as it seems. Logically, a serving of chips would be an individual bag, right? Wrong. Close reading of the label will usually reveal that the standard bag of chips is now really two servings! Eating processed, fatty, or salty foods is bad enough, but you're really eating more than you thought!

Nutrition Facts

Serving Size 2 oz. (56g/2/3 cup) Dry
Servings Per Container 8

Amount Per Serving

Calories 210   Calories From Fat 10

% **Daily Value***

Total Fat 1g	2%
Saturated Fat 0g	0%
Polyunsaturated Fat 0.5g	
Monounsaturated Fat 0g	
Cholesterol 0mg	0%
Sodium 0mg**	0%
Total Carbohydrate 42g	14%
Dietary Fiber 2g	8%
Sugars 3g	
Protein 7g	

Vitamin A 0%	•	Vitamin C	0%
Calcium 0%	•	Iron	10%
Thiamin 30%	•	Riboflavin	10%
Niacin 15%	•	Folate	30%

*Percent Daily Values are based on a 2,000 calorie diet.
Your daily values may be higher or lower depending
on your calorie needs.

		Calories	2,000	2,500
Total Fat	Less Than		65g	80g
Saturated Fat	Less Than		20g	25g
Cholesterol	Less Than		300mg	300mg
Sodium	Less Than		2400mg	2400mg
Total Carbohydrate			300g	375g
Dietary Fiber			25g	30g

Calories per gram Fat 9 • Carbohydrate 4 • Protein 4

The food label is an essential source of information to anyone who watches what she eats. Reading and understanding the label is part of taking responsibility and control of your body and your health.

How should you read the food label? Starting from the top of the label is the serving size. This will tell you exactly how much of the food makes up a serving. This lets you compare how much you really eat with what the FDA defines as one serving. For example, if you eat a whole box of macaroni and cheese (and I know that many of you do), double the number of calories, fat, or protein you see on the label, because double is what you are getting.

Moving on down the label, we come to the calories. This is the number of calories per serving. In the case of one box of macaroni and cheese, the serving size is only one cup (not the box). And across from the calories, the label will tell you how many of those calories come from fat. The FDA included this information because Americans consume too much fat, and most of our serious health issues are related to the high amounts of bad fat that we eat.

On the burger and cheese label, you will see that nearly half of the calories in one serving comes from fat. Since your goal is to keep fat intake to 30 percent or less, everybody's favorite Whopper and cheese turns out to be a high-fat food that everybody should avoid, or eat in small portions.

Next on the food label is the actual amounts of fat in grams, broken down into saturated, monounsaturated, and trans fats. The amount of cholesterol is also given. Then the amounts of sodium, carbohydrates, and fiber follow, and, on the right, what percent of your daily quota you're getting from that food. Next in order are protein, vitamins A and C, and the minerals calcium and iron.

For each item, at the far right, you'll see the percentage of your total recommended intake of that item. This percentage is based on a 2,000 calorie diet using the standard food pyramid. If you are not on a 2,000 calorie diet, or if you are diabetic or have other medical conditions, these values may change. For example, if you have high blood pressure, the sodium (or salt) that the label says is 23 percent of daily intake (540 mgs) may in fact be a much higher percentage of the amount you should really consume.

Notice that protein has no recommended daily value. That's because at present there is no evidence that protein intake is a public health issue.

For each category, your doctor and/or your dietician can help you figure out the right amount for you. Each person varies. For example, if you have gone through menopause or if you are a teenage girl, you will need more calcium than the standard daily recommendation.

So, although in most cases it is unnecessary to calculate exactly what percentage of calories you get from a serving of a particular food, the food label gives you at least a general idea of what, and how much, you are putting into your body.

Fast Food: Ultimate Saboteur of a Healthy Diet

There are so many things wrong with fast food I hardly know where to begin. The fast-food culture is a prime example of the three main reasons we are so fat:

- Extra large food portions,
- Convenience (that is, you don't have to work off calories to get it),
- Horrifically unhealthy food choices.

The junk-food industry uses a clever marketing scheme to suck us in and make us fat. The scheme is called "value marketing," and it means that the particular restaurant chain may charge less money for items grouped together as a meal than it does for items purchased separately. This makes purchases like huge hamburgers a "bargain." But the cost is high if you include the cost to your health.[4]

Here are a few examples. It costs 8 cents more to purchase one fast-food restaurant's quarter-pound hamburger with cheese, small fries, and a small soda separately than to buy the "extra value meal," which comes with the quarter-pound burger, large fries, and a large coke. But the extra-value meal rings in at 1,380 calories while the regular meal adds up to 890 calories, In short, cheaper is not necessarily better.

Convenience stores are also getting into the value marketing game. At one large, national chain a large soda will cost you 42 percent more than a smaller one. That means, you're encouraged to get 300 percent more calories! And when you go to the movies, the difference between a small bag of popcorn and a medium bag of popcorn is 71 cents. However, there are 500 more calories in a medium bag than in a small bag! So although the price only increased by 25 percent, the calories and fat increased by 125 percent.

So when we see a "bargain," we feel we have no choice but to take it. Who in their right mind would turn down more food? Why, that's un-American! And this is exactly why fast food is a straight shot to obesity and all the health problems that come with it.

The second way that fast food causes us to be fat is "convenience." Convenience means easy to reach, something that increases comfort and makes work less difficult. In other

---

4. We're happy to report that, as this book goes to press, McDonald's has announced that they will no longer market their "value meals."

words, the fast- food culture is one where you can drive up, order junk, eat it, and never leave your car. It takes no expenditure of energy, and the only calories burned are those used to chew.

The sad fact is that we have become a community of couch potatoes. Our children are dying because they don't move. They sit and watch TV or play Game Boy™ while munching on something that not only has no nutritional value but also hurts their heath.

Still more problems come from the fact that fast foods tend to be fried, and to contain heavy amounts of refined, processed carbohydrates (white bread, French fries, soda). That combination makes the typical fast food meal a death sentence waiting to happen. Besides what I've already told you, the calories these meals offer have a high glycemic index, so eating these foods causes big surges of insulin, and therefore more and more storage of fat.

Whoops! I almost forgot: fast foods (and other processed foods) are high in salt. If you have high blood pressure, heart, or kidney disease, this increased salt can cause major problems.

If you still have doubts about the health impact of fast foods, just look at the steady decline in other countries once the fast-food chains invaded their shores. Japan and other Asian countries historically have been the healthiest, with their people living unusually long lives with very low incidences of obesity-related illnesses. But now people in Asian cities can get fast foods just as easily as we can in the United States. Now they are reaching for their insulin, just as we are here. It goes without saying that the underlying cause is the rise of obesity.

Hey, it's me again. I'm going to tell you something honestly. (Not that the "Doc" isn't honest, she's just in a different space, ya know?)

Eating well is work. You really have to plan and grocery shop and cook. Unless you are a person who loves to shop and cook and try out new recipes, the work can seem not only time- consuming but boring.

Many people, once they get into cooking, love it, and learn to manage the necessary time. But even if you don't learn to love it, some things that we don't love to do we have to do anyway. I don't like going to the dentist, but I go because I don't want my teeth to fall out. So maybe if you're uninspired about the effort required for a good diet, you can think of it like I do. We'll just do it because the price of not doing it is just too high.

And another thing— I happen to LOVE fast food. In fact, a world in which I can't have a big burger with cheese or a two-piece fried chicken meal isn't a world I'm very interested in living in. That said, I've also realized that the time for me to have that burger or chicken isn't right now. Limiting the amount of fast food in my diet, and perhaps removing it until I'm healthy and fit, is definitely a modification I can make. Of course, the end result is worth it. And in case you're wondering, I'm just telling you all this so that if you see me one day in line at McDonald's for my once-a-month—or once every three months fix—please don't call me out! I'm still a work in progress.

That's great from Teri. But the reality remains that fast food is bad for your general health and won't help you reach your weight-loss goals. But this is the beauty of this book: we give you the information and you make your own choices.

Taking the time to cook at home takes diligence and work, but it pays off. To help make it a little easier, you can find easy, tasty, and healthy recipes at www.hiltonpub.com.

Chapter Eleven   *Exercise*

Now that you know what to eat and what not to eat, we have to turn to the second and equally important factor in the weight loss equation. You guessed it—exercise. No discussion about weight loss would be complete without it. Yes, I know how a lot of you feel about exercise, but please don't put the book down. You've come too far for that.

Most doctors think that exercise is *the* single most important thing anyone can do to improve his or her health. The benefits of exercise and physical activity could fill a book. Here's the short version.

If you have doubts about the benefits of exercise, check this out. Moderate exercise for thirty minutes each day

Most doctors think that exercise is the single most important thing anyone can do to improve his or her health.

- Helps to bring about weight loss and keep it off long-term
- Lowers blood pressure
- Improves the health of your heart
- Builds muscle mass, allowing you to burn calories easier and more effectively
- Strengthens your bones, making you less prone to osteoporosis
- Lowers the risk of diabetes and cancer
- Makes your body use sugar more effectively

And if all that doesn't make my case, try this:

Exercise increases production of "feel-good" chemicals in the brain called "endorphins." Endorphins make you feel calm and happy—and who can't benefit from a little more peace in their lives?

People get scared off by exercise, thinking that lots of expensive equipment or gym membership is required. Drop that notion. I believe that something, anything, is better than nothing, and the surgeon general of the United States agrees. Physical activity does not need to be strenuous for you to get some health benefit. Just by walking to the store instead of driving, or walking up two or three flights of stairs instead of taking the elevator, can help burn calories and improve weight loss. Granted, those activities aren't the optimal level of activity, but it's okay to start small, as long as you start.

Optimal physical activity means doing something that increases your heart rate and keeps it up for at least twenty minutes. Yes, this involves sweat, and huffing and puffing, It involves feeling sore in the morning once in a while. And, oh yes, it may involve getting your hair messed up. But people who do exercise find all that a small cost for the health benefits and for the experience everyone who exercises regularly can tell you about: they feel good.

If you are walking every day and not breaking a sweat, you're not doing much to lose weight. Optimally, if you're looking for weight loss, you should get some kind of physical activity for at least forty-five minutes four days a week. Notice the words "at least." Five days are better than four, six days are better than five. You get the picture.

Do as much as you can, as frequently as you can. Even if you have to start with ten minutes a day, while you work up to your goal, then just do it. No pill, no magic formula is a substitute for exercise. That may not be what you want to hear, but trust me. All the feel-good endorphins that are released when you exercise will soon have you craving physical activity like you once craved giant burgers. It takes a little time, but it will happen.

Exercise must become a priority in your life. No exceptions. When you are running short on time or you feel tired at the end of the day, exercise should not be the thing you decide to skip. When you are pressed for time in the morning, do you ever decide to skip the shower before work? Or forgo brushing your teeth because you are a bit fatigued? Obviously not, because these things are important to you and they are a part of your daily routine. This is exactly how your relationship with physical activity should be. Teri hates me right now, because she is by far the most exercise-averse person I know. But even the hopeless "lovers of leisure" (as my sister describes herself) can achieve deliverance with just a little effort.

Working out doesn't necessarily involve joining a gym or purchasing expensive equipment. Take a close look at your day, and at yourself, and then decide what kind of physical activity would be best for you and when. Sometimes, the answer will be obvious when you just take that look. For example, if you drive to work each day and park in the lot in front of your office building, why not park a few blocks away and walk to your office? This may require that you leave for work a few minutes earlier and return a few minutes later, but look at what you're gaining.

Another suggestion is to take the stairs instead of the elevator. That costs you nothing out of your day, and without even thinking about it, you incorporate physical activity into your schedule. You may even find that gradually you prefer using your legs when you can. After all, your body is made to be used, not to vegetate.

Walking is another helpful activity that does not require expensive equipment or membership. All it takes is a comfortable pair of walking shoes and some motivation. Walking at a brisk pace (three to four miles an hour) for forty-five minutes each day will help keep the pounds off and your heart, bones, and mind healthy.

I have to share something with you. I hate exercise almost as much as I love fast food. In fact, I quite proudly consider myself an expert "lounger." My natural state of being is sedentary—that is, still, and the best day I can imagine is spending all day at home moving between watching TV on the couch and reading in bed.

I can't begin to tell you the number of times I've started an exercise program and stopped. Or started a program—committing myself to working out four to five times a week—and ended up only working out twice a week. Everything else came first, so it was easy to put exercise on the back burner because I hate it so much.

But one day something really funny happened.

I'd always heard of the "exercise high"—the state that exercisers reach that makes them euphoric and happy and that keeps them exercising. But I used to believe it was a myth created by the exercise industry to make people buy equipment or running shoes or clothes.

Then one day, after really pushing it during my forty-five-minute walk on the treadmill, I felt like laughing. My entire body tingled and I became giddy—just like I do after a couple of glasses of champagne. On the subway going home, I caught myself smiling at strangers— knowing that they most likely thought I was crazy!

When I got home, I called Stacy. It felt so good I had to tell her all about it! And you can imagine how happy my news made her.

I've started exercising regularly. And although I haven't again reached the exercise "high"—the idea that I might one day get the "giggles" after a hard session on the treadmill keeps me pushing.

So no matter how you feel when you're sweating and straining to exercise, keep in the back of your mind that at some point, once your body adjusts to the pain, all of the work will make you feel great. The feeling is so good, in fact, that it's enough to make me   a die-hard, certified couch potato—keep working out consistently. Now THAT'S some drug!

I need to remind Teri, and you, of one hard truth: the older you get, the slower your metabolism becomes. No one is immune. This means that you cannot eat and exercise the same way forever without gaining weight. As time goes on, you must continue to increase the level and duration of your physical activity, while making small changes in your calorie intake.

But the bottom line is that the number-one predictor of long-term, long-lasting weight loss is exercise. Yes, if you cut enough calories, you will lose weight, but if your goal is to keep the pounds off and be healthy in the process, then exercise is the key.

Chapter Twelve   *If All Else Fails*

So what do you do if you have tried to exercise and to stay on a healthy diet but it's just not working? Tell your doctor. If your weight is a health risk, your doctor and you can find a plan that will work. Just keep trying!

There aren't many worthwhile things in life you can accomplish on the first try. Losing weight, like everything else, takes practice and experience. Are you a great mom? If the answer is yes, then think back to the first day you brought your little one home. It probably wasn't as smooth an experience as it is now. You practiced and you got good at it. Were you a first-rate driver the first time you got behind the wheel? Probably not. But you stuck with it, and the same is true with developing good exercise habits.

But if you and your doctor agree that you've done everything you can and it's not working, there are other alternatives, sometimes necessary. Keep in mind that these are extreme measures, either because of cost or actual risks. I'll list them, starting with the least extreme:

- Weight loss centers and programs
- Prescription medications
- Weight loss surgeries

Weight-Loss Centers

I put weight loss centers on my "extreme" list because it costs you a lot more money than the options I've already discussed. But a lot of people are spending that kind of money, so let's take a look at the programs. I'll let Teri kick this one off.

Back in 1995, I got ticked off. The demands of work and law school, coupled with late night snacking, eating out, partying, and fast food had taken its toll. I'd gained more weight.

I was not happy about it. Worse, my boyfriend at the time was not happy about it. Most painful of all, my mother was extremely unhappy about it. So I had to do something quick.

Enter a new plan that had helped some of my friends lose weight.

Unlike many other things that I'd tried, this program was steeped in moderation. You ate three meals a day with snacks. You checked in weekly with your counselor. And you lost weight.

All that sounded pretty good to me, so I tried it. What I learned is that such plans require a lot of time. You're expected to eat the pre-planned foods that they have carefully measured and cooked. But often a week's supply of food would sit in the freezer for weeks— simply because I wasn't home to eat it.

It was the old problem—overbusy-ness. That, plus I like to go out to eat with my friends. There was no way I could do that and strictly stick to the program. I kept gaining weight, and the food stayed in my freezer. I don't say that it won't work for others, but for me it was costly and I couldn't make it fit into my daily schedule.

I am usually a cynic when it comes to commercialized weight loss programs. I think there are many deceptive people who are out to take advantage of the fears and desperation of others. They promise the world, tell you what you want to hear, take all your money, and in the end, leave you bigger and unhealthier than you were when you started. That being said, I have found some very positive aspects of these programs.

Group or team weight loss plans are a popular and often successful means of weight control. In the United States, while the names of the leading programs are different, the basic premise is similar: to provide a more personalized, healthier approach to weight loss.

Most of these programs focus on long-term weight management, with the goal being to lose 1 to 2 pounds per week (which is very medically sound). They also provide consultants who are a combination of "diet coach" and personal motivator. Further, these programs provide other life-management strategies, such as stress reduction, and the need to come to terms with the psychological reasons behind your overeating and obesity. Usually the programs are structured within group meetings, regularly scheduled, where people can get strength from others who are in the same (very large) boat.

As for the actual meals and diet plans, they are usually based on the United States Department of Agriculture's food pyramid. This means that typically the plans are low in fat, with the majority of calories coming from carbohydrates. However, some centers are offering higher protein and lower carbohydrate plans in response to the growing trends of diets such as Atkins. The programs stress that variety in what you eat helps you to stay on the program by limiting boredom and recurrent food cravings.

Another aspect of these programs that I especially like is that they teach you to understand the meaning of the word "portion." Most of you reading this just discovered what a true portion size is only a few pages ago!

One of these programs uses what they call a "point system," in which all foods are given a point value based on the number of calories, the amount of fat, and the amount of fiber they contain. This applies not only to the packaged diet food but to all the food you eat. For example, a slice of pizza is worth nine points and a beer is three points. You are allowed a certain number of points a day, but you can eat whatever you like as long as you stay within the daily point range.

On the whole, except for the people whose menu is pizza and beer, or something of the sort, here is a diet that can work because it helps to limit boredom, gives a lot of variety; and makes use of your psychological understanding both to motivate you and to help you understand the reasons you eat too much.

The negatives, to remind you, are that these programs

- May be hard to fit into your schedule.
- May be more expensive than they seem at first glance, once you add the cost of the pre-packaged meals and the cost of the meetings, usually once a week.

Medical professionals, such as registered dieticians, nurses, and sometimes physicians, ordinarily run weight loss centers, which is a good thing. And the programs do provide some counseling about exercise, physical activity, and changing the habits that made you fat in the first place. Their main emphasis, however, is on food choices.

In the end, I'd say that these programs are medically safe and worth a try for those who want more structure and group support for their efforts. The key benefit from these programs and your ultimate success will only be realized if you take the lessons on portion control, food choices, and healthy lifestyle, and apply them at home once the program has ended. If you can pass those good habits on to your kids and loved ones as well, it will more than pay off!

Prescription Drugs

So what do you do if the weight loss centers just don't work for you? You've "Been there. Done that." Well, you still have options for jump-starting your weight loss. But remember the more extreme the measures, the more risk.

Prescription weight loss drugs are usually the next level people turn to when "old-fashioned" plans have failed. Don't make such an important a decision on your own. You're just playing with fire. Buying prescription drugs off the Internet, from Mexico, or from your cousin Ray is gambling with your health— and maybe your life. Prescription drugs can have serious side effects that need to be monitored by a doctor.

So begin by talking to your doctor. Listen to the cons along with the pros. Your doctor won't prescribe such medications if, for example, you have high blood pressure or other forms of heart disease. Weight-loss pills are appropriate only if the risk of continued obesity is greater that the risk of the medication.

With one exception, weight loss medications are controlled substances—meaning that you need a special type of prescription and the DEA (Drug Enforcement Agency) carefully monitors its use. You should be glad of that (remember the Fen-Phen® disaster).

Today, most prescribed diet medications work by changing your brain chemistry to make you feel full. This family of drugs includes Subutramine (or Meridia®) and Phentermine (trade names are Fastin®, Adipex-P®, and others).

There are two main chemicals in your brain that affect your mood and appetite. These are serotonin and catecholamines. Don't worry about the long names; just be aware that these drugs do affect important body functions. Since they are serious drugs, the side effects can be serious as well. The drugs can cause increased heart rates and increased blood pressure, which can be dangerous in those people with hypertension, a history of heart attack or stroke, or heart rhythm irregularities.

You can see why I insist that these drugs be considered only if exercise and diet alone have not been effective and the risks of your continued obesity are greater than the risks of the medication. And even then, you should take these drugs only under the supervision of a doctor, who will frequently monitor your blood pressure and heart rhythm.

Abuse (meaning getting hooked on the drug) is uncommon with prescription appetite suppressants unless the drug contains amphetamines, but still, if you have a history of alcohol or drug dependency, avoid these medications.

The one major prescription weight loss medication on the market today that is not an appetite suppressant and does not act on the chemicals in your brain is called orlistat (or Xenical®). This medication works by cutting back on the amount of fat that is absorbed in your body. So when you eat a meal containing, for example, 30 grams of fat, if you are taking orlistat, only 20 grams of fat are actually processed. By reducing fat absorption by a third, you will be decreasing fat calories and, therefore, weight loss can potentially occur.

The excess fat is eliminated through the gastrointestinal tract. If you take orlistat, you will likely have a lot of gas with oily spotting and fatty stools. There may also be some fecal incontinence, meaning you may not be able to control your bowels.

These side effects are usually only temporary, but they get worse as you eat more fat. A burger and fries will result in more oily, gassy, fatty stools than a meal of veggies. That effect can encourage weight loss because you tend to avoid foods that cause the discomfort. So you may not be much fun at parties, but the side effects, though annoying and sometimes uncomfortable, are not injurious.

Because orlistat reduces the absorption of some vitamins and nutrients as well, you should take a multivitamin supplement while on the drug.

Once you've decided to look into either family of drugs, the first step is a visit to your doctor. If your doctor simply writes you a prescription, turn around, walk out the door, and find another doctor, because the one you have is dangerous!

Your physician should first take an extensive health history and perform a physical exam. Lab tests should be done, and special attention should be paid to blood pressure, other risk factors for heart disease, and whether you have a family history of heart disease. Your doctor should also determine exactly how overweight you are by calculating your BMI (that's Body Mass Index, remember?) and getting your waist-to-hip ratio.

Remember, if it is more than 0.8, it means you are at an increased risk for all the bad stuff, such as diabetes and heart disease.

When the physical examination and lab samples are complete, your doctor should have a serious discussion about your weight history, what diets you have tried in the past, what your goals are, and how serious you are. The primary goal in starting these medications should be to improve your health and to reduce the risk of serious disease, not to get into a thong by summer. "Behavior modification" is still the main goal of the program—in other words, you must still exercise and make changes in your eating habits.

What you probably expect from these prescription weight loss drugs is usually much more than what you can realistically achieve. These medicines are modestly effective when used with an exercise and diet plan, but don't expect to reach your goal weight with the pills alone.

Different people respond differently to the drugs. Maximum weight loss, if it happens, occurs at around six months. You should stop using the drugs after six months in any case. But if these drugs are going to work, you usually know over the first four weeks, when you should lose at least four pounds. If you don't, then the chances that you will respond later are slim.

After treatment with these medicines, your weight will generally increase, unless you have developed an aggressive exercise and diet plan. So these pills are not "magic bullets." They are simply a "jump start" for a select group of obese individuals, but they are nothing without the changes in behavior that must be a part of your life forever if you are to remain healthy.

Nip 'N Tuck

The most drastic treatment for severe obesity is surgery. Surgical options are not for everyone. There can be serious, potentially life-threatening complications, so patients must be carefully selected.

Who would make a good candidate? To begin, you have to be big. Really big. Surgery is not an option for those who want to drop an additional 40 pounds. Or even 50. It is for those morbidly obese people who need to lose, on average, at least 100 pounds. BMI should also be in the 40 range as well.

Ordinarily, a candidate for weight-reduction surgery is already suffering from obesity-related health complications, such as diabetes, high blood pressure, or sleep apnea. The presence of these illnesses shows that the obesity has developed to such a point that the dangers of the fat outweigh (no pun intended) the risks of the surgery.

Traditional methods of weight loss should have been attempted. Often, however, candidates for surgery are too obese to even begin an exercise program, so their metabolism remains at a standstill and the weight continues to pile on.

There are two main types of weight loss surgeries: stomach restrictive surgeries (where the stomach is reduced in size), and gastrointestinal bypass surgeries (where a part of the bowel is skipped over).

The most widely used type of stomach restrictive surgery is the vertical banded gastroplasty. It is commonly referred to as "stomach stapling." It works because the size of the stomach is reduced to a pouch that can hold only about one tablespoon (or 15 ml) of fat at a time. Naturally, a person who has had this surgery will typically get a sensation of fullness after eating only a little, but if you try to eat more than this markedly smaller stomach can hold, nausea, vomiting, and pain can result. This is a big deterrent to overeating, so the weight loss is achieved due to very diminished calorie intake. However, exercise remains a critical part of the long-term program.

Complications of this procedure include infection (as with any surgery) or blockage of the outlet portion of the stomach—if the stapling is too tight). Correcting this problem requires more surgery.

Another possible complication is that, because of the combination of being obese and being bed-ridden after surgery, blood clots can form in the legs or in the lungs. The first case is not extremely serious, but clots in the lungs can be deadly. Death rarely occurs because of the surgery itself, although it is possible. The very best way to prevent complications due to surgery is to choose a doctor who has a lot of experience in performing the procedure.

Once you get beyond the surgery and hospitalization and finally get home, other complications can arise. These include vomiting that may be hard to control. Also, after the surgery, a large portion of the stomach is no longer available to absorb the vitamins and nutrients, so you must take vitamins and supplements.

Like every other possible treatment for obesity, this surgery is not a "magic bullet." Anyone considering the surgery must be reminded that they also have to make long-term changes in eating habits. Even after surgery, you can still gain weight if you consume high-calorie foods and liquids, such as ice cream and soda. That is why it is not just a reduction in the amount of food that causes weight loss after surgery, but also a change in what you are eating as well.

The average weight loss following vertical banded gastroplasty is 50 to 100 pounds, but patients lose even more weight if they exercise and are careful about what they eat.

In mid-2001, a new weight loss surgery, laparoscopic gastric banding was approved. This procedure is similar to the vertical banded gastroplasty but is done in a less invasive manner. In this surgery, an adjustable band is placed around the upper part of the stomach. This effectively creates a much smaller stomach, so less food can be consumed at a sitting and you lose weight.

This surgery is done laparoscopically, meaning that instead of opening up your abdomen as required with the vertical banded gastroplasty, the surgeon uses a special device with a camera on the end, called a "laparoscope." Small incisions (roughly half an inch across) are made on the stomach, and the surgical instruments are passed through these small holes. The camera allows the surgeon to see what he or she is doing.

Because you are not "opened up," the healing time is remarkably fast and the risk of side effects is much lower. However, there can still be the usual complications. This surgery is technically more difficult than vertical banded gastroplasty, so it is vital that you find a surgeon who is skilled and experienced in the procedure.

The two procedures I have described are both stomach restrictive surgeries. Another type of surgery is the gastrointestinal bypass. Bypass surgeries are still more complicated and extensive. At the same time, they usually result in more weight loss.

What happens during the operation is somewhat complex, but I'm going to give it a shot and watch my sister cringe in the process. First, the size of the stomach is reduced by stapling across the top of it. That's the easy part. Next, a piece of the small intestine is cut and brought up and attached to that smaller piece of stomach. You still with me? Good. What this does is to make the stomach smaller so you can eat less food at any one time. It also bypasses a portion of the small intestine so that there is less absorption of the food you do eat.

The initial results from such surgery are usually excellent: 50-60 percent of the excess body weight. Further, people who have had bypass surgery are more likely to maintain these dramatic results than people who have had the stomach stapling procedure.

Naturally, there is a down side. There are more potentially severe complications and side effects from the bypass operation. Not only is the stomach drastically reduced, but a good part of the small bowel is eliminated from the process of digestion, thus patients are more likely to experience vitamin deficiencies and have problems with digestion.

Further, because the surgery itself is more complex, the risks of the procedure are also greater. So you enjoy quicker recovery but risk more severe complications.

Forgive me, but I can't say it too often: for *any* weight loss treatment to be successful, you must change your habits and the way you live. Not even weight loss surgery is a sure bet. What causes you to lose pounds is not the surgery itself but the restrictive diet that results (ideally, along with exercise). So if you want to save yourself a lot of money, just follow around a person who has had the surgery and eat what she eats. You will lose weight almost as quickly as she does.

I know that there are so many promises, so many possibilities, that sometimes it's hard to choose the one that's right for you. Some people, out of that confusion, choose to pursue fads, gimmicks, and all types of magical thinking. But I want to help you see your eating habits and dietary decisions from a new perspective. Think about this: If you drink a regular soda for lunch once a day, you are adding on fifteen pounds a year. Simply eliminating that soda will cause you to drop over a pound a month without even trying!

A glazed donut every morning for breakfast? How about thirty pounds a year! So even the little things can add up. Wasn't that simple?

I am going to leave you with some parting thoughts:

1. Don't forget your common sense. Try not to fall for the quick fix. This journey is not just about losing enough weight to fit into the bikini. It's about changing your life and your behaviors forever. There's no quick and easy fix.

2. See your doctor. Before beginning any weight loss plan, check in with your physician. Get a physical, discuss your optimal weight, and get help from your medical professional. Your doctor should help you figure out a diet plan or refer you to a dietician for more help.

3. You must eat to live. Starvation isn't healthy. You need regular meals throughout the day in order for your body to burn calories effectively and to have energy for physical activity.

4. Move! Move! Move! You must exercise regularly for healthy weight loss to occur. There is no way around it. Exercise must become a habit and a priority. Learn to love it.

5. Portions! Portions! Portions! Get your scale and measuring cup, and plan your meals based on what an actual serving is.

6. Read Labels. Know the content of the things you are putting into your temple. You are what you eat, so if you're eating junk. . . .

7. Fast Food. *Forget about it!*

8. Relax. Life may have its ups and downs, and your battle with obesity will bring you good days and bad days. But take it one step at a time, and with a little patience and dedication, anything is possible.

9. Fix your head first. If you are blaming your weight problem on things you can't control, like your bad genes or a silent metabolic problem, you are considering yourself a victim and have already lost the battle. You have to realize and accept that it's your body, your health, and your responsibility.

And finally, number 10—just do the damn thing!

Chapter Thirteen
What Victory Looks Like

You've spent quite a bit of time reading about all the things that can go wrong when you're too heavy. You've also read about my own experiences and other people's. And you've read about what you should and shouldn't do if you want to achieve a healthy weight. Now, finally, it's time to show you what victory looks like. It happens to look just like my Ernesha.

To put it simply, Ernesha is a strong, bright life force. She's the kind of person who walks into a room and stops everything. We joke with her all the time about her having a "red phone" directly to the Lord! She's wonderful—and things just seem to go her way.

Ernesha grew up in a strong family, filled with love. Her parents are still together, and her siblings all get along. That much she inherited. The rest she made on her own. She is smart and beautiful and hardworking and fun and good.

But when I met Ernesha, she weighed over 300 pounds. You're not going to believe me, but on Ernesha, the weight was almost unnoticeable. What people did notice was her rich personality and soul.

It's not that Ernesha herself had ignored her weight. Like most of us with weight problems, she had tried all of the diets and cleanses and programs that she could find. She'd always been "thick," but her real weight problem started ten years ago. That's when she moved to New York City after college, and gained more than 100 pounds because she was in a new environment, far away from her usual support system, and dreadfully lonely and bored. So she ate, and ate, and ate.

Ernesha didn't think of her weight as a problem until her father had a major heart attack. He was also diabetic. Mr. Webb survived with the help of good medicine and lots of love.

After having to face her father's mortality, Ernesha decided she also had to face her own. That's why, a week before Thanksgiving, 2001, Ernesha went to her first Weight Watchers™ meeting. A few weeks later some friends, including me, joined her. The friends came and went and came again, but Ernesha just kept on going.

To people like me, who saw her every day, the change was hardly noticeable. But gradually, we did notice a few things. For example, Ernesha 's cheekbones, long buried, were beginning to show again.

Happy with her accomplishment with Weight Watchers™, Ernesha started working out. Nothing huge. But almost every day, no matter what, she went to the park and walked. She shocked us all when we learned that she liked walking so much that she'd started jogging. She'd also joined a gym and started weight training.

Her goal? "Tankini, 2003."

You see, Ernesha's thirtieth birthday was coming up in March, 2003—the party was to be in Miami—and the goal was for her to be fit enough to wear (and look good in!) a two-piece tankini swimsuit.

Some people were skeptical. Some people criticized her goal as unrealistic. Some people simply thought it was just talk.

But those who knew Ernesha best knew that it was a challenge she had made to herself. And we knew that Ernesha never gave her word to something without coming through. The longer she stayed on the plan, the harder she worked. She worked so hard, in fact, that even the best cake in Brooklyn couldn't force her off track!

I mean, I'm talking about the best cake! In Brooklyn, there's a bakery called "Cake Man Raven." Cake Man sells the most perfect red velvet cake ever made and sells it by the huge slice. So I'm talking about temptation.

Well, one Sunday afternoon Ernesha, along with all of the girls, had a piece of cake from the Cake Man. And when her roommate and friend A'Donna came home after dark that Sunday night, what did she find? Ernesha. In the dark. Outside, in front of their apartment building. On the sidewalk. Jumping rope.

You laugh. But that is how dedicated she was. Even the occasional slice of Cake Man's cake couldn't deter her from the big goal.

For those of us who knew and loved her, the amount of weight she just kept losing never really sank in. But one late afternoon at a Weight Watcher's¹ᴹ program that I actually did attend, I saw Ernesha step on the scale—and she was down eighty-nine pounds!!!

I wish you could have seen her face. She was proud and happy and amazed at the work she had put in, and the results she had achieved. And everyone there was proud of her.

But she wasn't done.

Next were the 5K walk/runs and training for a mini-marathon. Exercise was now a brand new part of her reality. She got stronger and healthier and lighter. I wish we could tell you that Ernesha changed. But she didn't. Who she was stayed exactly the same—she was the person that she was when she started back in November, 2001. She was the daughter of Ernest and Katie. Devoted sister. Loving friend. And it was those qualities that she had from the beginning that kept her going even when the results were slow and the work was hard.

Ernesha lost weight without gimmicks. She did it with nothing more and nothing less than dedication, hard work and tons of prayer. She chose her new habits and her new lifestyle. The reward was a better body.

And on March 30, 2003? Miami Beach—Ernesha wore a black and white tankini.

In my mind's eye, I see her on the beach: the shining image of victory.

This is as close to a fairy tale ending as you can get!

At this point, you've traveled with us for a while and are armed with the information you need in order to make good choices. With these choices, you have everything you need to create your own fairy tale ending.

So now it's just a question of moving forward and doing all that we can. Sure, until your new lifestyle becomes second nature, every day may be a struggle. But here's the thing—as long as you commit to moving forward and doing better, you win! And so does your family and the people you love and who love you. On top of all that, your community and race also wins.

At this point, I guess the long argument between Dr. Stacy and struggling Teri is over. We've come to the same conclusions. We do so as two African American women and sisters trying to make our way in a world that isn't always perfect, but a world with endless possibilities.

There is work to be done—in our individual lives, in our homes, in our communities. And in order to do it, we have to be ready—mentally, emotionally, and physically. Like Ernesha, we recognize that weight is the very least of what we are. But we must also recognize that excess weight can keep us from doing the real work we were put here to do.

So even if you don't remember about BMI and apnea and hypertension, and have to look them up in the index over and over again, there's one big thing we most hope you *do* remember: you *always* have a choice. You have a choice today to do something different from yesterday. This very minute you can choose to do something different from what you've done before. Life is a sequence of such moments, like a puzzle made up of little pieces. A lot of good "little pieces" will make a good life.

The most important things in our lives—friendships and family and love—require nothing more than the choice of our presence. And what better gift can we give ourselves and our loved ones than being present at our absolute best?

Tomorrow is guaranteed to no one, so choose to be your best. Today. With love.

Index

191